"Do you think anybody will want to read about me?"

THE LAST QUEEN OF JAIPUR

The legendary life of H.R.H. Maharani Gayatri Devi

Text Dharmendar Kanwar

Editorial project Valeria Manferto De Fabianis

Editorial coordination Laura Accomazzo

Graphic layout Patrizia Balocco Lovisetti

Contents

The Editor wishes to thank the "Sawai Jai Singh Benevolent Trust" for their invaluable help without which this book could never have been realized.

Special thanks to Mila Bertinetti and Marcello Libra for their fundamental contribution to the project by finding and reproducing the documents and photographs of H.R.H. Maharani Gayatri Devi.

Sincere thanks also to Sudhir and Sanjai Kasliwal of the Gem Palace in Jaipur for their much appreciated and indispensable help.

Preface

I am very happy that a pictorial book is being published to mark my 90th year. I am not sure that people will want to read this book but I can see that a lot of effort has gone into compiling it and it is done very well.

I hope this book provides a glimpse into my life and the kind of activities that were part of the olden days. Those were different times and I don't think that there are too many people of my generation left who have lived through that era. The generation of today takes a lot of things for granted, especially in the field of education, but the 30s and 40s were a period when we had to make a lot of effort to ensure that there was education for all, especially women. When I got married and came to Jaipur in 1940 His Highness said I should do something to eradicate the prevailing purdah system here and I said to him: "Give me a school and I'll be able to do it." Fortunately, I was able to do that when I started MGD School within three years of my marriage.

Dharmendar, who has written this book, has been a student of my school and I have known her for almost thirty years. She is the Secretary of the Sawai Jai Singh Benevolent Trust, started by the late His Highness, and being a writer I depend on her to assist me with all media-related work. In all these years of close interaction I have grown quite fond of her and enjoy her company tremendously. I often seek her advice on a lot of matters as she is very balanced and always gives me the most practical advice.

I am happy that she has written this book on me because she has been closely associated with me, she has travelled with me and seen me in a lot of different situations; she knows and understands me very well.

People keep asking me if there are any unfulfilled dreams or any regrets and I can only say that I am very happy with the way I have lived my life and have no regrets whatsoever nor do I have any unfinished work that I need to complete.

Rajmata Gayatri Devi of Jaipur

Introduction

"Do you think anybody will want to read about me?" asked Rajmata Gayatri Devi of Jaipur when I was working on this book and then answered the question herself: "Nobody will buy the book!"

Coming from a woman who was known the world over for her beauty and has been considered the ultimate in style and grace you would think that she was being flippant, but she was not. She genuinely believed that people may not want to know about her life! She was undoubtedly a legend in her lifetime but sometimes you did wonder if she was aware that even up to the age of 90 her strong and forceful personality, her inimitable charm and grace were still intact. Just a few minutes in her presence were enough to understand why she had been idolized over the years. What an amazing woman she was. Courageous and charismatic, she led a really fascinating life.

Since the Forties she was a much written and talked about Maharani. As students of her famous Maharani Gayatri Devi Girls Public School we have always admired and idolized our founder. The highlight of our school days was when this extraordinarily attractive Maharani visited the school. For gawky teenagers, as most of us were, she was like a vision from some fairy tale. We ran from our classes at the slightest pretext and walked past the Principal's office to catch a glimpse of her. Just seeing her from afar was enough, being in the same room with her or talking to her was unimaginable. If she looked at one of us and gave a half smile, it was a matter of great pride – and envy for the rest. This extraordinary lady continued to mesmerize people all her life. People often made the mistake of thinking of her only as 'one of the most beautiful women in the world' She was more than just a pretty face and though many found it difficult to associate her with social reform and other such concrete issues hers was been a long and eventful journey, and one that revolutionized life in Jaipur.

I first met her for some writing assignment given to me by the Principal of MGD School. Then there were interviews for other magazines and more writing projects that kept me in contact with her. In 1979 she asked me to assist her in compiling a book on her husband, the late Maharaja Sawai Man Singh II of Jaipur. The project had to be abandoned for several reasons but I continued to meet her. Later, I got involved with the restoration of old historical monuments in Jaipur and given her interest in preserving the building heritage of her favorite city there was greater interaction between us. She happily accompanied me to monuments like *Nahargarh* and *Maharani Ki Chhatri* to see the restoration work in progress and gave very valuable suggestions. Her profound interest in the city never ceased to amaze me. She wrote to concerned officials and thought nothing of accompanying them personally on drives through the walled city to point out encroachments, hoardings and other eyesores. In May 2008, just two days before she left for England, she did exactly that. She invited the Mayor of Jaipur to drive around the walled city with her and expressed her concern at the pitiable condition of the facades and filth of the city's streets. The fact that within a week after this trip the Mayor took it up as a personal mission and gave the necessary orders to remove the hoardings and encroachments shows how much her approval was valued and sought after.

My association with her dates back to the late 70s and I followed her life very closely all these years. When we discussed the possibility of doing another book on her she agreed a little reluctantly but then decided that I would be the most suitable person for this job. She probably felt that I would not take too much of her time in gathering the required information as I already had several hours of interviews on tape and had met a lot of people associated with her.

Writing about the life of Rajmata Gayatri Devi of Jaipur could be a writer's dream – or nightmare, depending on how one looks at it. A dream: because hers has been an extraordinary life and gathering information about it was like coming in close contact with history and getting a glimpse into her world peopled by legendary figures such as Gurudev Ravindra Nath Tagore, C. Rajgopalacharya, John and Jackie Kennedy, Pandit Nehru, Dr.

Bhimrao Ambedkar, Sarojini Naidu, Queen Elizabeth and Prince Philip, the Mountbattens and many more. A nightmare: because so much has been written about her that it makes one wonder if there is anything new that you can add that hasn't already been said about a hundred times before? But *A Princess Remembers* does not mention the incredible courage that she displayed after she lost her husband and son, maintaining her grace and dignity in the face of personal trials and tribulations. Or that she was raising funds to strengthen the agencies involved in protecting the heritage of the city; helping to provide a more suitable shelter for the elephants in Jaipur; contributing to the shifting of villages located in the core area of the Ranthambhore National Park; or helping to build a new school for the physically challenged children. The honest truth is that hers was such a multi-dimensional personality that at times it was very difficult to be objective.

But can any *one* book ever do justice to her?

Working on this book wasn't without its fiery moments. When she read a few pages of the text, her reaction was "This is all wrong! All this never happened. How do you know this?" No amount of convincing worked, "Is this your life or mine? I know better…this is all untrue. …..Don't argue with me." One fiery meeting followed another and when I looked very troubled both Maharaj Jai Singh (Joey) and Maharaj Prithvi Raj Singh (Pat) would smile knowingly and ask, tongue in cheek, 'So are you enjoying working with the most difficult person in the world ?' or 'What have you gone and done today? You've spoilt her mood early in the morning!' Rani Vidya Devi, the wife of Maharaj Jai Singh was a constant support and always listened patiently when I grumbled about the problems I had in getting information or some related problem.

The daily morning recording sessions (sometimes evenings) became a habit; it was something that I looked forward to. It was a chance to get to know her better and see a more humane side in everyday situations. Her sense of humor, her kindness and compassion and her love for her beloved Jaipur all come through very strongly. A few years ago when she appointed me as the Secretary of her Sawai Jai Singh Benevolent Trust and I also took on the role of her media advisor I had the unenviable job of checking her when she blithely went about distributing rare photographs and letters and getting into difficult situations with publishers. I would request her not to commit to anything without first consulting with me and for a few days she would remember to do that. Once I was in Agra for a couple of days and she called me up to ask if she could give some of her pictures to a publisher. She said, "I'm asking you otherwise you'll scold me!" Scold her? Would I dare?!

For me it has been an honor to have worked with her so closely and I shall always treasure the memories of the time spent with her. The beauty of her mind and spirit has touched my life in more ways than I can express and if I have been able to give you even a tiny glimpse of her indomitable spirit then I have been successful.

My one regret will be that this book could not be published during her lifetime. But knowing her she must be looking down with a big smile on her face and thinking, "Will anybody want to read this book?!"

DHARMENDAR KANWAR

A MAGICAL CHILDHOOD

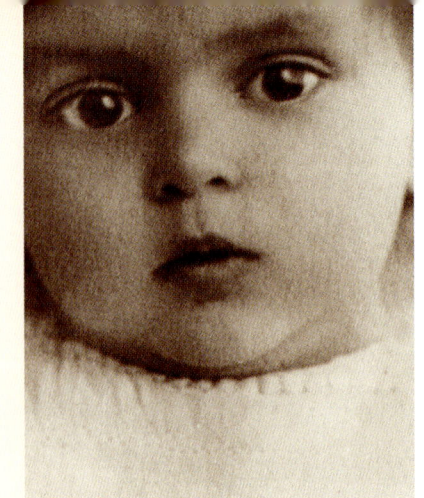

1919-1929

Gayatri Devi came from a westernised family where womenfolk were educated, independent and had a mind of their own and she inherited these qualities from them so she wasn't really doing anything unusual or deliberately shocking.

16 Ayesha was born in London but spent her childhood between India and England. This photograph shows the young princess aged two, in Cooch Behar.

19 Ayesha's mother, the beautiful Indira Raje formally dressed in traditional clothes, poses with her mother, Maharani Chimnabai of Baroda.

20 left There was never a dull moment in Baroda. Picture shows Indira Raje's mother Maharani Chimnabai playing the *veena* and various relatives relaxing in the huge gardens of the palace.

20 right Ayesha's grandfather, Colonel HH Sir Nripendra Narayan Bhup, Maharaja of Cooch Behar (1862–1911) was acknowledged as the architect of the modern city of Cooch Behar. He was responsible for the construction of various buildings for administrative purposes.

It's a cliché, but there can be no better beginning to this book than the one Richard Bach wrote for *Love Story* several years ago – *"What does one say about the most beautiful woman in the world?"* And what does one say about a woman who continues to be a legend in her life time – a woman who continues to fascinate people to this day.

Hers has been a life so rich and enthralling that no matter how hard you try to recount her fascinating story it would still fall short of doing justice to her persona. It's a fairy tale peopled by kings and queens, presidents and prime ministers, Hollywood stars and the crème de la crème from all over the world. Today, in her 90th year, Rajmata (Queen Mother) Gayatri Devi, better known the world over as Maharani Gayatri Devi, still looks as serene and graceful as she must have done in her younger days. The years have created delicate lines of age across her face, the passing years have also left their mark on her health but the indomitable spirit remains unbroken. She remains, without doubt, the most admired person in Jaipur today.

In the mid 1960s, she was internationally recognized as one of the world's most beautiful women, but she was a favorite of society columnists and photographers the world over much before that. She didn't need a magazine to acknowledge this fact. She was a fashion icon for several generations of Rajput women who emulated her gracious and iconic style of dressing – the famous pastel chiffons and her preferred string of pearls had become a hallmark of classic dressing in the late Forties and Fifties. And not just a fashion icon; as the third wife of the dashing, polo-playing Maharaja of Jaipur, Sawai Man Singh II, she was a livewire who took the old, staid Jaipur state by its horns and turned it upside down. Nothing was ever the same again. City elders were shocked by her westernized lifestyle. The previous two Maharanis were orthodox and rooted in tradition but here was a Maharani who moved around without *purdah*, drove her own car, wore trousers, played tennis and badminton and went horse riding.

This behavior seemed strange to the Rajput nobility of the 1940s but the young and high-spirited Maharani Gayatri Devi thought nothing of it.

21 The Laxmi Vilas Palace of Baroda was one of the most imposing palaces of its time. Picture shows the majestic Darbar Hall of the Baroda palace.

She came from a westernized family where womenfolk were educated, independent and had a mind of their own and she inherited these qualities from them, so she wasn't really doing anything unusual or deliberately shocking. Her mother, the beautiful and vivacious Indira Devi of Baroda had also been rebellious and came from a family of educated and revolutionary people. Indira's parents Sayaji Rao III Gaekwar and Maharani Chimnabai of Baroda insured that Indira Devi, their only daughter, was well-educated and as a result of this she became one of the first Indian princesses to receive formal education and graduate from Baroda College. The young Indira Devi also travelled to Europe frequently with her parents and was equally exposed to western culture. This independent streak in her came to the fore when her father decided to marry her off to the Maharaja Scindia of Gwalior. She rebelled and made it clear that she did not wish to marry him.

Rajmata says, "When my mother announced that she could not marry the Maharaja of Gwalior, there was a lot of confusion. Of course, she had nothing against the prince but she did not wish to be married into an orthodox household, and the chosen groom was 20 years older than her. It wasn't an instantaneous decision because she was engaged for a year and had even started her trousseau shopping in England!"

Perhaps what helped her to be firm in her decision was the fact that she had fallen in love with Maharaja Jitendra Bhup Narayan Bahadur of Cooch Behar, a young prince from the east whom she had met in 1911 at the Delhi Durbar. The family was shocked, more so because not only was Baroda a bigger kingdom, which was entitled to a 21-gun salute, but also because Jitendra was not the Maharaja of Cooch Behar, a remote state in the eastern hills, but the younger son (and thus unlikely ever to become king).

Even though the family tried to persuade Indira not to be stubborn she remained in contact with Jitendra Narayan, and exchanged letters and met him whenever an opportunity arose. Though matters of state kept Sayaji Rao busy he was worried about his daughter as he feared that she might take a drastic step to avoid getting married to Maharaja Scindia. She was kept under close scrutiny but it did not really help matters because Indira was adamant.

After two years she took matters into her own hands and wrote to her fiancé saying that she did not wish to marry him; a daring act for an 18-year-old Indian maiden of that era. In Baroda, Indira's father received a single-sentence telegram from the Maharaja of Gwalior: *"What does the princess mean by her letter?"* Indira's parents were stunned, for them it was a matter of great disgrace and they were hard put to extract themselves from this situation in an honorable way.

Fortunately for them the Maharaja of Gwalior eased their apprehension by reacting to the unexpected turn of events in an exemplary fashion.

24 top The enormous palace of Cooch Behar was constructed in 1870 by an English architect and consisted of two great wings that flanked a great central hall.

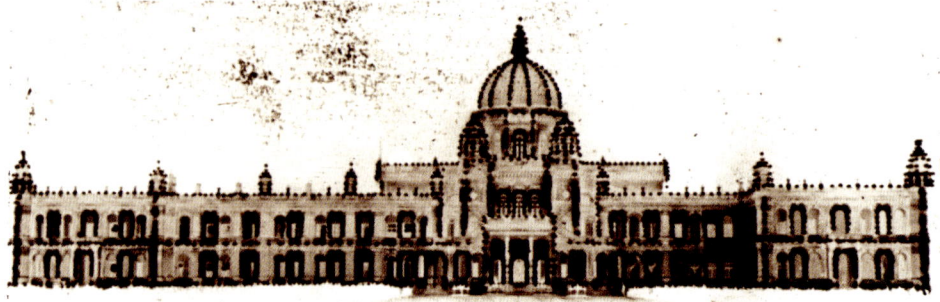

He wrote a very understanding letter to Sayaji Rao which he signed off as "your son", however, the helpless parents could not reconcile to this ignominy and it took them a very long time to accept their daughter's refusal and subsequent marriage to the prince of Cooch Behar.

The engagement was called off but Indira's parents did not wish to step back and let their daughter go ahead with her plans without trying to drill some sense into her. It did not help because both Indira and Jitendra were equally adamant. Eventually, perhaps also in recognition of the fact that Indira would not relent, her parents made a half-way compromise. They allowed Indira to proceed to London and marry her chosen beau.

When Indira Devi went to say goodbye to her mother, the Maharani sat quietly and did not respond to Indira Devi's emotional farewell nor did she show any sign of affection. Indira Devi could only cry and stammer incoherently before she left. When her distraught daughter left the room, the Maharani could not control her feelings anymore and wept as though her heart would break.

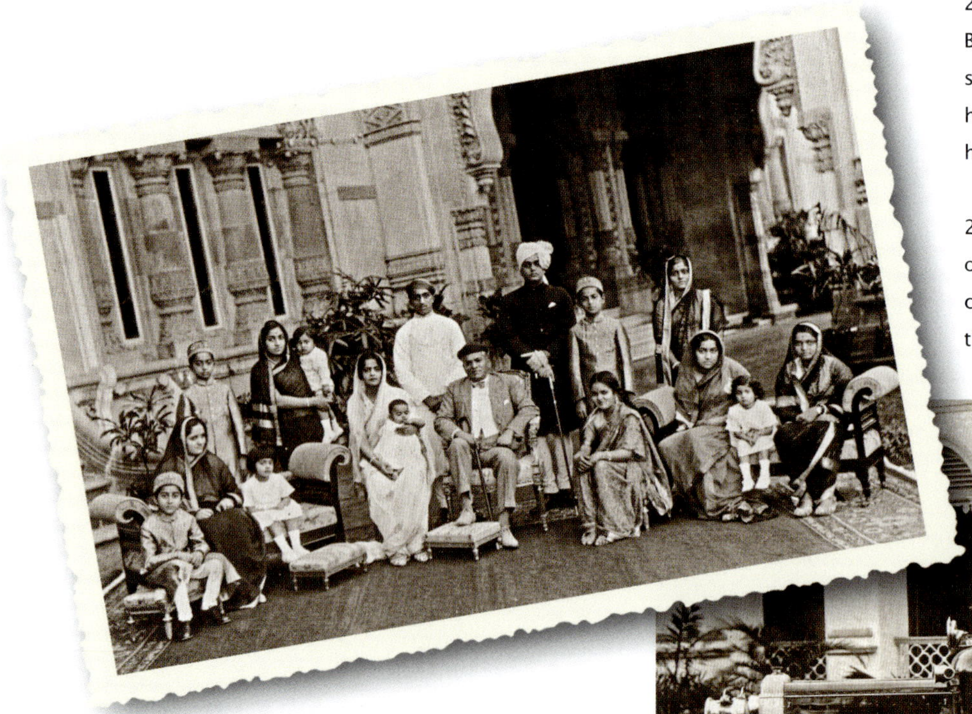

24 center Indira Devi visited her parents' home in Baroda regularly even though the relationship was strained for a while after she chose to marry against her father's wishes. Picture shows Indira Devi with her father and other members of her Baroda family.

24 bottom Maharaja Jitendra Narayan Bhup Bahadur of Cooch Behar, Ayesha's father, in his State car escorted by his ADC and driver, outside Woodlands, their residence in Calcutta.

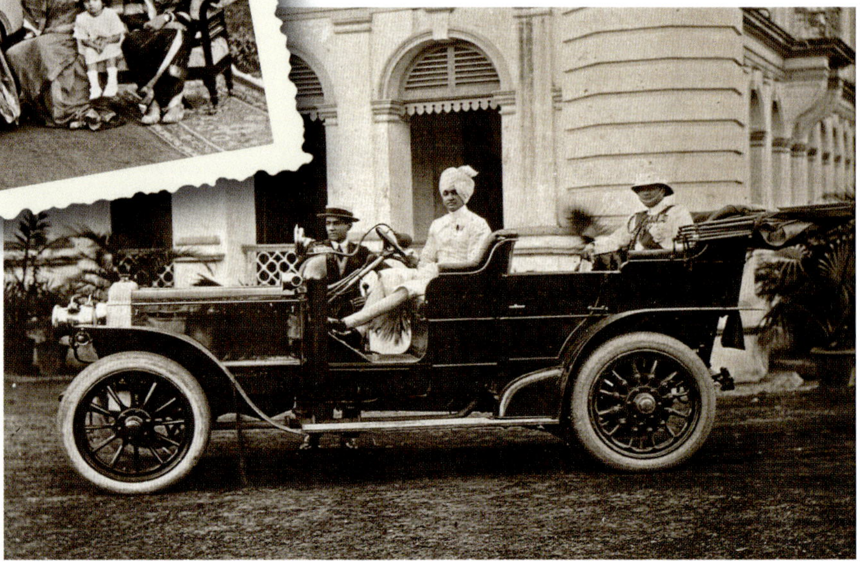

25 The Cooch Behar children - Raj Rajendra Narayan Bhup Bahadur (standing fourth from left), younger brother (Ayesha's father) Jitendra Narayan Bhup Bahadur (extreme right) and other cousins.

26 There was very little age difference between the three sisters – Ila was the oldest one followed by Ayesha, as Gayatri Devi was known, and the youngest Menaka. Picture shows the three sisters posing for a photograph in Cooch Behar.

27 Ayesha as a baby, photographed in London, where she was born. Photo below shows Ila Devi and Bhaiya posing in Cooch Behar.

"Grandmother really loved her daughter and wanted her to be happy but the situation prevented her from saying anything to her. She looked extremely stern but underneath lay a heart of gold," says Rajmata of her maternal grandmother.

All opposition had been overcome and Indira and Jitendra were wed in London on August 25, 1913 but with no member of Indira's family present for the big occasion; representing her side of the family was her mother's companion and lady-in-waiting Miss Tottenham. It was a simple and short ceremony as they were wed by the rites of the Brahmo Samaj, the sect to which Jitendra's mother, Sunity Devi, a daughter of Keshab Chandra Sen belonged. This was followed by a trip to the registry office where their marriage was also solemnized according to British civil rites.

The young couple was blissfully happy and after a brief honeymoon Indira Devi moved to her home in Cooch Behar, in October 1913. Their honeymoon plans had to be changed slightly when Raj Rajendra Narayan, the Maharaja of Cooch Behar, and older brother of Jitendra, died in a nursing home in London after a brief illness. So three weeks after his marriage to Indira Devi, Jitendra, being the eldest of the surviving brothers, became the Maharaja of Cooch Behar.

When the newly married couple returned to Cooch Behar it was amidst great rejoicing and they were given a traditional welcome befitting the new *maharaja* and *maharani*. Jitendra Narayan assumed the duties of the new ruler and as a devoted and car-

ing husband he did not neglect his duties towards his 21-year-old bride. Their first child, a daughter, Ila Devi was born in October 1914, she was followed a year later by Maharajkumar Jagaddipendra Narayan, better known as Bhaiya, born in 1915, and another son Maharajkumar Indrajitendra Narayan in 1918. Everything seemed to be going well for the Cooch Behars but Jitendra Narayan's health began to give way and he had to travel to London for treatment. The family of five was in England when the fourth child, Gayatri Devi, better known as Ayesha, was born on May 23, 1919.

The two names confused people for a long time. "In the early years people used to question me about my name but there was really no great mystery behind it. I was called Ayesha simply because my mother had been reading Rider Haggard's novel *She* and had liked the book and its heroine so much that she decided that if a girl was born she would call her Ayesha, after the heroine of the book. I was born in England but my horoscope was cast in India after the time difference had been adjusted by the pundits and they picked the auspicious letter 'G' for my name," recalls Rajmata Gayatri Devi.

She was followed by Maharajkumari Menaka Devi in 1920. The family was now complete, and the passing years had also thawed the cold war between mother Chimnabai and daughter Indira Devi and they began communicating more frequently after the children arrived.

28 and 28-29 Even as a little baby Ayesha looked adorable. This photograph was taken in Cooch Behar and gives a hint of the supreme confidence that went on to become a hallmark of her style! Picture on the right shows all the Cooch Behar children together with the youngest, Menaka, lying in front.

30 left The beautiful princess Indira Devi of Baroda photographed in the early Thirties as the incredibly stylish Maharani of Cooch Behar. She had an innate sense of dress.

30 right and 31 Maharaja Jitendra Narayan Bhup Bahadur of Cooch Behar photographed in England in the 1920s. He is surrounded by all his children, the young Ayesha is seated behind her father. Picture on the right also shows the entire family in England. Ayesha's father, Maharaja Jitendra Narayan Bhup Bahadur of Cooch Behar ascended the throne in 1913 after the premature death of his older brother, the Maharaja Shri Raj Rajendra Narayan Bhup Bahadur.

Unfortunately, Jitendra Narayan did not recover from his illness and died on his 36th birthday, December 20, 1922, merely nine years after his marriage. Indira Devi was devastated and sailed back to India a few weeks later with her children.

Rajmata recalls, "I don't remember my father because I was only three years old when he died but I do know that it wasn't easy for my mother to bring up the children on her own. Though she was a strong woman it must still have been a daunting task but she took it on with great courage and a sense of duty."

In 1923, the eldest born son Bhaiya – Jagaddipendra Narayan, a mere eight-year-old child, became the Maharaja of Cooch Behar and the 30-year-old Indira Devi was installed as the Regent for her son. In those days it was the usual practice to appoint a Regent and a Minority Council and there was no better person than Ma Cooch Behar to be given this respon-

sibility. Ma was an incredible woman and handled her duties and responsibilities admirably. It couldn't have been an easy job with five children on her hands and State matters to attend to.

But the traveling continued – sometimes for work and sometimes for pleasure. So much so that England was almost like a second home to the Cooch Behars. The early years of Gayatri Devi's life were spent there and she and her other siblings were looked after by English nannies and governesses. Looking back at those early years she says, "We attended many schools in England, France and then India because my mother was worried that Bhaiya would get spoilt if he grew up in Cooch Behar. This fear was further strengthened when she noticed that he was never declared 'out' when he played cricket with the local boys!" He was sent to St. Cyprian's Prep School and the two younger girls were sent to Glendower, a day-school in London. Gayatri Devi and her younger sister Menaka were the

my family

only Indian pupils and quite awkward in their ways initially. They were familiar with the language but not quite used to formal English schoolrooms and mannerisms and the fact that they were young princesses also made them stand apart.

Just as they were beginning to get used to their purple uniforms and the school, Ma Cooch Behar decided it was too cold in England and moved to Le Touquet in France.

Rajmata remembers that her mother had an intriguing social life that was filled with partying and the most interesting friends. She was seen at all the stylish places across Europe. She also had a great reputation for entertaining and threw the most lavish parties that were the talk of the town. An incredibly beautiful woman, she was remembered by a close friend thus: "To describe her beauty as ravishing would by no means be using an overworked cliché. Reporters flocked to our home,

endless photographs were taken and we small boys lived in a haze of reflected glory." A fact confirmed by her family though as children they never thought of her looks. Rajmata herself recalls, "You know she was the one who started the trend of wearing chiffon saris. She had them made especially in France, it was her style that was emulated by women across the country. In fact, I find it so difficult, even now, to talk about my mother's beauty, we just took her looks for granted. I do remember, however, that my resemblance to her was quite striking because the Viceroy, Lord Erwin used to call me Second Her Highness. She was, without doubt, one of the most amazingly beautiful and exciting women that I have known."

Ma Cooch Behar's grace and charm continued to fascinate people but she could not sustain herself or her family when her luck ran out after she lost a huge sum of money on the gambling tables, and they moved back to England.

32-33 As the Cooch Behar siblings were growing up they were quite at ease with photography sessions that were a regular feature. In this interesting composition Maneka, Indrajit, Ila, Jagaddipendra and Ayesha pose in their informal clothes.

A year later it was time to move again, this time to Switzerland. In 1929 Menaka Devi fell ill and had to be sent to a sanatorium at Leysin, in Switzerland and Gayatri Devi and Baby, (daughter of General Khusro Jung, the guardian of the five Cooch Behar children), a childhood companion, went to a nearby school called Les Noisetiers.

It was a French school and for the English and Bangla speaking young ladies it was an altogether interesting experience trying to come to terms with yet another new school and a new language.

Ma had been away from Cooch Behar for almost 15 months and very soon there was pressure from the Government of India for her to return to the State and fulfill her duties. So the family headed homewards again.

As a result of this constant moving from one country to another the Cooch Behar children had an amazing childhood. "You must understand that given my mother's lifestyle we had to do a lot of traveling. She wanted us to be with her so we grew up in England, France, Switzerland and India! But at least we were together. Changing schools was not such a problem because either Menaka or Baby was with me. We were familiar with the language and our western upbringing had ensured that we were never out of place in these situations. However, many times I did wish that I didn't have to go to so many schools," recalls Rajmata.

It is not surprising that Ma Cooch Behar was the first and the most enduring influence on the young princess. She seemed to surpass in every-

34 When the Maharaja of Cooch Behar died in 1922, the young Jagad-dipendra Narayan Bhup Bahadur was crowned Maharaja of Cooch Behar at the tender age of seven.

35 The young Ayesha was more of a tomboy and hated to dress up in formal clothes but as a princess she did have to follow certain norms. Here she is seen dressed as a proper young princess.

thing that she took on from parties to the décor of the palace and all other palatial homes that they lived in.

Rajmata says, "She excelled in decorating and arranging the house and we had the most beautiful homes in Cooch Behar, Calcutta and Darjeeling. She loved collecting objets d'art wherever she went. There was furniture from England and France, fabric and chandeliers from Italy, rugs from Kashmir and so on. She had great taste and the palaces were a reflection of her taste and personality."

The grandchildren also remember her immaculate style. Devika Devi, Ila Devi's daughter and also Rajmata's daughter-in-law who was married to Maharaj Prithvi Raj Singh, endorses this, "Grandmother was very particular not only about the décor of the rooms but also and how they must be readied for guests. She also personally checked every little detail – about each pillow, each light and each writing table in the rooms. In the 21 guest bedrooms that the palace had she knew where each flower vase was to be placed and what flowers were to be put in each of them."

The palace has now been acquired by the Archaeological Survey of India and turned into a museum but Rajmata continues to take keen interest in it and visits it each time she's in Cooch Behar because the palace holds a lot of happy memories for her. "We had the most wonderful childhood possible, there was so much activity there, so many young cousins and a constant stream of visitors that kept us amused," says Rajmata of those early years.

Innocent childhood years that were not overly affected by the freedom struggle that had begun to sweep over the entire country.

THE ARRIVAL OF PRINCE CHARMING

1930-1940

Gayatri Devi was a mere child of 11 when the struggle for *swaraj* or the freedom movement was at its peak throughout the country. Mahatma Gandhi and Jawaharlal Nehru were at the helm of this struggle against British imperialism and had launched a civil disobedience movement throughout the country.

36 In this picture, taken several years before her marriage, the young Ayesha is formally dressed in a sari with a simple string of pearls.

39 Ayesha as a carefree, young school girl with windblown hair... difficult to imagine that this young girl would go on to become one of the most beautiful women in the world!

40 Indira Devi was a frequent traveler and was often accompanied by her children or other members of her family. Top she is seen at the airport with her children and an ADC. Bottom left: An exercise book that was used by Ayesha when she was studying in Santineketan. These simple books were in use throughout the country and used for taking down notes. Bottom right: Darjeeling was special for Ayesha and she has fond memories of the time spent there with member of the family as well as friends who were based in Darjeeling. Picture shows her with a family friend.

41 Life in Cooch Behar was great fun when all the siblings were together; there were a lot of bonding and shared activities; here the two brothers and three sisters are seen on the steps of the large Cooch Behar palace.

Such was the nationalist zeal that thousands of young students, even those educated in England, switched to *Swadeshi*, or the use of Indian goods and took an active part in picketing shops selling foreign items. Women across the country broke the traditional *purdah* and joined the freedom fighters in defying the British government.

In Cooch Behar, the children did not remain untouched by the rapidly growing influence of the freedom struggle. As proud nationalists they had their own spinning wheels and idolized Mahatma Gandhi and Jawaharlal Nehru as their heroes. They often joined their servants' children in shouting anti-British slogans.

Though Cooch Behar was located in the eastern corner of the country it did not miss any of the turbulence that was ripping through the country. Not far from their State were Calcutta and Chittagong (now in Bangladesh)

that were home to several freedom fighters who kept the movement alive. But it was Indira Devi's paternal home that seemed to be in the thick of things. Her father Sayaji Rao refused to be cowed down by British dominance. He demanded greater independence from their stifling control and showed his displeasure at being treated like a minion, which he was not. Therefore it was not a surprise when he publicly praised Mahatma Gandhi; he showed his support when, on March 12, 1930 Gandhi started his Civil Disobedience Movement and together with 78 chosen followers, crossed his state en route to Dandi during his famed Salt March to protest against the British salt tax.

Indira's mother Chimnabai was equally firm in maintaining her grace and dignity when dealing with the British dignitaries. Though good friends with Lord Willingdon who took over as Viceroy in April 1931, there are ac-

Going there was always for the whole winter holiday on the Lloyd Triestino ship 'Biancamano'. I used to love those voyages by sea and would make all over the ship — climb up to the crow's nest. I'd be everywhere and make friends with everyone.

42 and 43 top Darjeeling was a favorite summer destination and the entire family spent a lot of time there. Picture shows Ayesha playing with her pet dogs.

43 bottom Playing all manner of sports was among the various activities that kept the children busy. Picture shows Ayesha and her older sister Ila Devi relaxing after a game of tennis.

counts that record the fact that she once went to visit Lady Willingdon in Delhi but refused to alight from her car until the Lady herself came out to receive her!

This period of unrest was marked by attempts on both sides, Indian as well as British, to come to some kind of understanding and three major Round Table Conferences were held to resolve the strife.

Throughout this period Indira Devi's life followed her chosen pattern of traveling between Europe and India and she resisted all efforts by the Indian Government to rein her activities. The Cooch Behars had a beautiful home in Calcutta called Woodlands and summer retreats in Darjeeling and Ooty. As the family moved, according to the season and occasion, the retinue of staff also moved with them. Through it all the Cooch Behar children moved between these continents and attended new schools, met new people and made new friends but Indira Devi insured that their education

never suffered. Two governesses, Miss Oliphant and Miss Hobart were employed to teach the children French, German and English while two local teachers were on hand to teach them all the other subjects.

When the children were not being given tuition they were involved in a wide range of activities that usually centred on *shikar* (hunting) and sports. Ila was 16, Bhaiya a year younger and Indrajit was 14. The two younger princesses Ayesha and Menaka were 11 and 10 respectively and more focused on playing rather than getting involved with the parties or the celebrities that attended them. For them there was more fun in riding elephants and playing with the children of the staff rather than being impressed by the countless important guests who visited Cooch Behar.

Gayatri Devi and Menaka spent hours playing and getting into all kinds of mischief typical of young kids. Gayatri Devi also shared a room with Menaka. "Unlike me Menaka was quite a proper young lady, she kept her side of the room very neat and tidy," recalls Rajmata. "I was a real tomboy and quite happy in pajamas and loose, comfortable tunics while Menaka loved to dress up and wear jewels."

Menaka was mild tempered and doesn't recall having any serious fights with her older sibling, "Oh she was quite gentle with me and we never really had any great fights, just minor arguments over toys or things like that. She was a tomboy but we used to spend hours playing in the huge doll's house that was in the rear grounds of the Cooch Behar Palace."

The sheer size of Cooch Behar palace necessitated the presence of enough staff for the smooth running of affairs; there were plenty of grounds for riding, cricket, croquet, tennis and parties. There were ladies-in-waiting, gardeners, cooks, butlers, store keepers, cleaning staff, personal maids, ADCs, secretaries, tutors, and other staff to ensure that each department of the palace functioned smoothly whether it was the *shikar* department or one that took care of the elephants and the horses. The children had their own favorites amongst this fleet of around 400 staff. A particular storekeeper was liked because he sneaked a chocolate to one of the children if they happened to be in the vicinity; a favorite butler told them interesting stories, listened to their complaints or played with them. Some were admired and some were teased for their mannerisms.

Along with the fun and games that seemed to be the main attraction for the young children, they were given training in horse-riding and tennis while the boys played hockey, cricket and football. Shooting was another skill that all the children acquired from a very young age. Gayatri Devi went for her first *shikar* at the age of five and by the time she was 12 she had shot her first panther. Gayatri Devi remembers the event very clearly, "Indrajit, Menaka and I set off after lunch, each of us on elephants, accompanied by an ADC and other members of the staff. Very soon we heard the elephants trumpeting as they usually did when they sensed the presence of a wild animal in the vicinity. When the panther was forced out of cover and stood right in front of my elephant, the ADC behind me told me to shoot."

Showing remarkable presence of mind and a firm control over the 20-bore gun, Gayatri Devi got the panther in the face with the first shot. It was a landmark event and there was much jubilation and the young princess was congratulated by the entire group. Gayatri Devi recalls the excitement and the sense of pride that she felt after this achievement, "Ma was in Delhi while both Ila and Bhaiya were away in school, but everybody at the palace congratulated me and made a big fuss over me. We sent a telegram to Ma and told her about it."

44 and 45 The lush jungles of Cooch Behar were ideal for *shikar* camps and picnics. There was a full-scale *shikar* department that organized these events and looked into every little detail to ensure that everything went smoothly. Pictures show a line-up of elephants with hunters astride looking for game; Ayesha with her prized catch and on the right a *shikar* party in progress. The young Ayesha is first on the left and Indira Devi is in the middle towards the left.

46 The huge grounds surrounding the Cooch Behar palace were put to good use by the children who were fond of outdoor activities. These included all manner of sports such as horse riding, polo, tennis, cricket and badminton. Picture on top shows Ayesha and her brother with a guest on horseback. Bottom: Ayesha and Menaka with their governess after a game of tennis.

46–47 and 47 bottom Ayesha had a great love for horses and loved riding. She was an excellent horse rider and it was this common interest that she shared with her future husband that brought them together. Pictures show her clearing a hurdle with great ease.

Maharaja Man Singh

The year 1931 was special for another reason. It was the year that Maharaja Man Singh of Jaipur (better known among friends as Jai – short for Jaipur) first visited the Cooch Behars when he came to Calcutta to play polo. Woodlands was a hive of activity and Ma Cooch Behar threw some of the most lavish and sought after parties. "Woodlands was always full of people. I remember some of them like the Maharaja of Kashmir, Prince Aly Khan, Douglas Fairbanks Sr. and of course the most glamorous visitor of all the Maharaja of Jaipur. In fact, when Menaka and I had to give up our rooms to him we did not mind the inconvenience at all because the prospect of a visit from such a hero was a more exciting prospect!" says Gayatri Devi.

It wasn't just Gayatri Devi who considered the Maharaja of Jaipur a dashing hero. Other people also agreed. Rosita Forbes, an English writer of that period wrote about him thus:

"Because of his appearance and his charm, his possessions and his feats on horseback, this exceedingly good-looking young man, famous as a sportsman in three continents, occupies in the imagination of the Indi-

an general public much the same position as the Prince of Wales did in the minds of working men (in England). In no way can I suggest the universal popularity, combined with the rather breathless wonder as to what he will do next, which surrounds this best-known of India's young Rulers."

In the young Gayatri Devi's eyes he was a hero who swept her off her feet. He spent a lot of time with the family and even took her out a couple of times. Being a sports loving person herself she found him even more attractive. She started to daydream about him and wished she could spend more time with her Prince Charming.

The idyllic days were interrupted when Ma Cooch Behar decided to send her elder daughters to an Indian school where they would come in closer contact with Indian traditions and also be able to converse in Bangla, their mother tongue. An ideal place, not too far from Cooch Behar was Gurudev Rabindra Nath Tagore's progressive countryside school, Santiniketan, set up in 1901. It seemed the best place for them to imbibe the values and traditional Indian culture that she felt was necessary for them.

48 Sawai Madhopur, located around 180 km from Jaipur, was a favourite hunting ground for the royal family of Jaipur. Pictures show hunting camps in Sawai Madhopur.

49 Thakur Sawai Singh of Isarda with his son, the young Maharaja Man Singh. Even though he had been adopted by Maharaja Madho Singh of Jaipur, Man Singh maintained close ties with his biological father.

50 and 50–51 The *shikar* camps organized by the Jaipur royal family were very popular with their friends and they waited to be invited to Sawai Madhopur for these camps. Pictures show a tiger being carried away by attendants; a picnic in progress and guests posing for a picture.

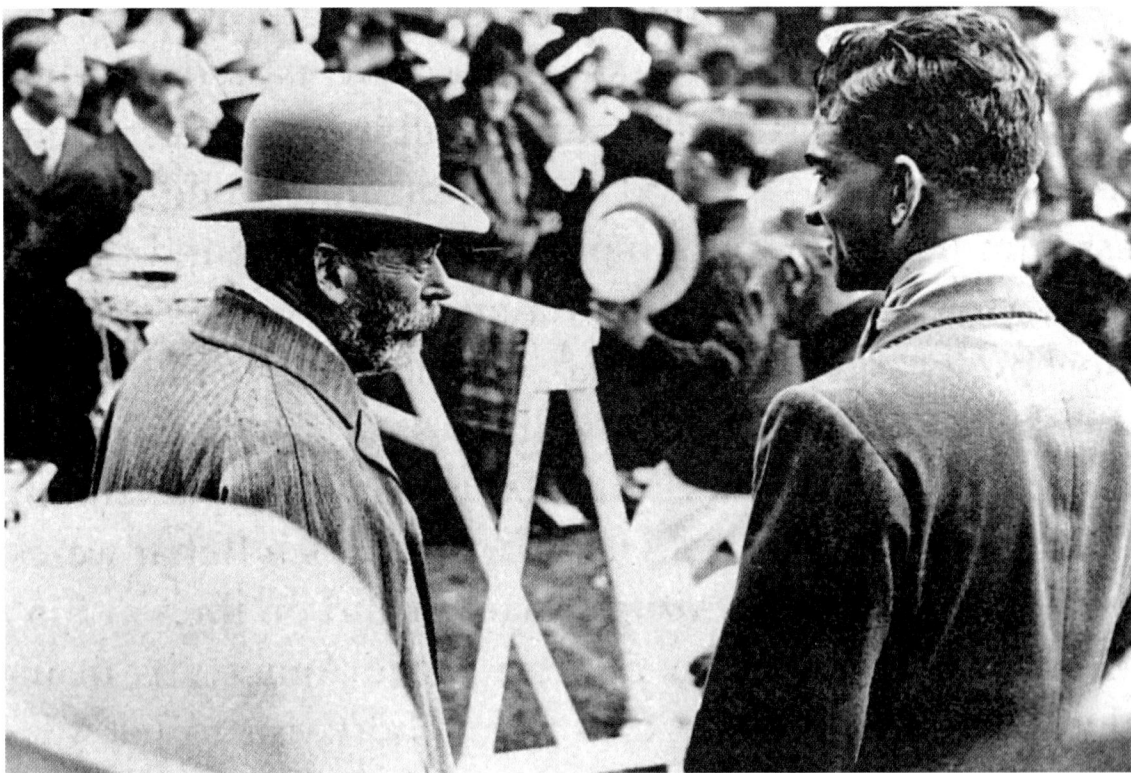

52 Love of horses and polo had the young Maharaja Man Singh traveling all over the world with his polo team. Most of the matches that the Jaipur polo team played had them walking away as the winners. Picture on top shows Man Singh with other members of his polo team with trophies in hand; picture below shows Man Singh sharing a word with King George V.

53 Wherever Maharaja Man Singh could play polo he carried his polo gear with him. Here he is seen in Ooty, South India with his polo gear – polo sticks, hats and the polo ponies in the background.

54 and 55 The Jaipur Polo team led by Maharaja Man Singh was recognized as the top polo team in the world, a team dreaded by most of their opponents. They were looked upon with awe and admiration and the newspapers and magazines acknowledged their mastery. Pictures show some newspaper cuttings of that period.

Country Life 15-7-33

Photo by]   TWO OF THE FINEST DEFENSIVE PLAYERS IN MODERN POLO.   [*Sport and G*
Major J. F. Harrison, of the Osmaston team, and the Maharaja of Jaipur. Here they are seen in the final of the Champion Cup at Hurlingham.

...er to drain both recepta...es...
...er, and the health of the M... f...
...out spilling a drop. To do...
...e time of Charles II.
...shaped "Bodkin" Cup, of silver...
...work. It bears a London hall-ma...
...mpet-shaped; the foot is relieved...
...reminiscent of a rose window, a...
...en of the Middle Ages.
...splendid Grace Cup, given by Kin...
...geons, was, originally, of about the s...

CURRENT TOPICS.

Our Visitors from India.

The Maharaja of Jaipur states that according to present arrangements his team will return to India in September. In all probability the team will play at Minehead at the close of the London season. Their visit has been one of the happiest features of the sporting year. Apart from their superb polo the Indian players have endeared themselves to all by their good sportsmanship and charm of manner. Nobody who followed their play in the tournaments for the Ranelagh Open Cup and the Champion Cup is likely to forget their delightful horsemanship—which seemed to enable each Jaipur player to reach the ball a trifle quicker than the other man—their perfect stick-work and their clever combination, these qualities making the highest honours of the season almost a foregone conclusion for them. Each member of the team has pulled his weight in the boat which has borne them to one triumph after another. Jaipur's success in the Roehampton Cup on July 8th gave them a complete sweep of the open tournaments.

Photo by]   [*Sport and General.*
PRESENTATION OF THE RANELAGH OPEN CUP.
General Sir Bindon Blood hands the trophy to the Maharaja of Jaipur, captain of the Indian team.

Morning Post 17-7-33

Polo: JAIPUR EASY WINNERS OF THE CORONATION CUP

THE KING AND QUEEN AT RANELAGH

The King and Queen on Saturday honoured the Ranelagh Club with a visit, and witnessed the final of the King's Coronation Cup tournament. After the match, in which Jaipur beat the Royal Scots Greys by nine goals to five, the Queen presented the cup to the Maharaja of Jaipur.

This tournament, which is the "championship of the champions," resolved itself into a single match, as the only two teams qualified this season to play for the cup were the Royal Scots Greys, winners of the Inter-Regimental, and Jaipur, the latter having won the Champion Cup, the Ranelagh Open Cup, and the Roehampton Open Cup. The game was preceded by a parade of 38 of Jaipur's splendid stud of ponies. Although they were meeting a much stronger side, whom they had no reasonable hope of beating, the Greys put up a plucky fight, but had it been necessary Jaipur could doubtless have increased their winning margin.

The Indian players made certain of the result in the first two chukkers, in which they scored eight goals to none, and at half-time they were leading by 8—1. The Greys, for whom Messrs. Guinness and Findlay were prominent, did well in the later stages, but Jaipur's ultimate success was never in doubt.

For the winners Abbey Singh scored five times, and Prithi Singh and Hanut Singh twice each. Findlay hit four of the Greys' goals and Guinness the other. Jaipur's next appearance will be on Wednesday, when they compete at Hurlingham for the Prince of Wales' Empire Cup. Sides:

Jaipur—Rajkumar Prithi Singh, Rao Raja Abbey Singh, Rao Raja Hanut Singh, and the Maharaja of Jaipur (back).
Royal Scots Grays—M. H. E. Lopes, R. L. Findlay, H. P. Guinness, and Major C. H. Gaisford St. Lawrence (back).

Times 17-7-33

The King and Queen were present at Ranelagh for the polo match for the King's Coronation Cup. It was won by the Maharajah of Jaipur's team, who beat the Royal Scots Greys by nine goals to five. The Queen presented the cup to the Maharajah of Jaipur after the match.

Details and reports will be found on the sporting pages and pictures on page 16.

Daily Mirror 17-7-33

HOUSEWIVES
...age 10 will be of in-
...aders.
...ckets of Symington's
...ween now and July 31.
...packet of Symington's
...ese sweets the house-
...of varying the summer

THE KING WATCHES POLO.—The King and Queen standing in the rain to acknowledge cheers at Ranelagh, where they saw the polo final for the King's Coronation Cup. The Maharaja of Jaipur's team beat the Royal Scots Greys 9—5.

ERS

They prevent
...g after staying

Look for this
Trade Mark
on every package

The Wonderful School Days

The girls set off for Santiniketan in 1934, and it opened a whole new world to them. Used to the stylish upper class schools of England and Switzerland, they were happy to come to a totally Indian atmosphere that brought them closer to their roots. Students gathered under trees for their classes as Tagore believed in open-air education rather than confining students in classrooms. The students also dressed mainly in traditional Indian clothes, ate Indian meals, sang Indian songs, in fact every aspect of this

wonderful institute presented an innate Indianness that appealed to the young princesses. They made an effort to mix with the other students though it did take them a while to be accepted as more than just princesses. As was the norm, an ADC, his family and a maid for the princesses accompanied them. Though Gayatri Devi slept in the dormitory with the other girls there was a maid on hand to do her odd jobs. Gayatri Devi stayed

58 School time in England was fun-filled as Ayesha was able to go to the countryside with friends and family.

59 Schooling in England meant that during vacations the young Ayesha had to head homewards to India. During those days the preferred mode of travel was by ship. Picture shows her sailing back to India.

in Santiniketan for almost a year and was happy with the chance it gave her to meet with other youngsters from diverse backgrounds. She recalls those days with great fondness, "I did go and meet Gurudev once in a while and I remember that he tried his best to make me behave like a proper young lady…he encouraged me to dance and participate in what were considered more ladylike activities. Gurudev was a little disappointed in me, I think, because I had to drop out of dancing because it clashed with my tennis timings. I preferred tennis to dancing!" The young princess was a tomboy and continued to behave like one.

While Gayatri Devi moved back to Cooch Behar in 1935 to sit her matriculation exam (which she passed with distinction), her older sister, Ila Devi, stayed on in Santiniketan where she met and fell in love with a fellow student, a young boy from Tripura. Fearing that Ma Cooch Behar would not approve, she married him secretly on June 12, 1936 and returned to Cooch Behar without revealing her newly acquired marital status.

Schooling over, Ma Cooch Behar wondered how she could keep her daughters busy. She wasn't too happy with Gayatri Devi's growing friend-ship with Jai, the Maharaja of Jaipur and felt that she was too young to be thus involved, even though Ma was very fond of the young Maharaja who shared her interest in horses. Jai became a frequent visitor to their homes in Calcutta, Darjeeling, Cooch Behar as well as England. He was young, rich and looking for some relief from his duties as a ruler; he needed to be in the company of people with whom he could let his guard down. He came from a State where women maintained *purdah* and the young Jai was understandably very impressed with the glamorous, educated and beauti-ful Ma Cooch Behar and her family as they provided the kind of compan-ionship that he yearned for.

This constant interaction made it difficult for the young Gayatri Devi and Jai to keep out of each other's way. Not that they wanted to or even tried.

Ma Cooch Behar was perceptive enough to understand why the young Maharaja was showing so much interest in Gayatri Devi and also knew that she was too young to know her mind. She didn't want her to get romanti-cally involved at such an impressionable age. Eventually, she decided to send her off to a finishing school in Switzerland.

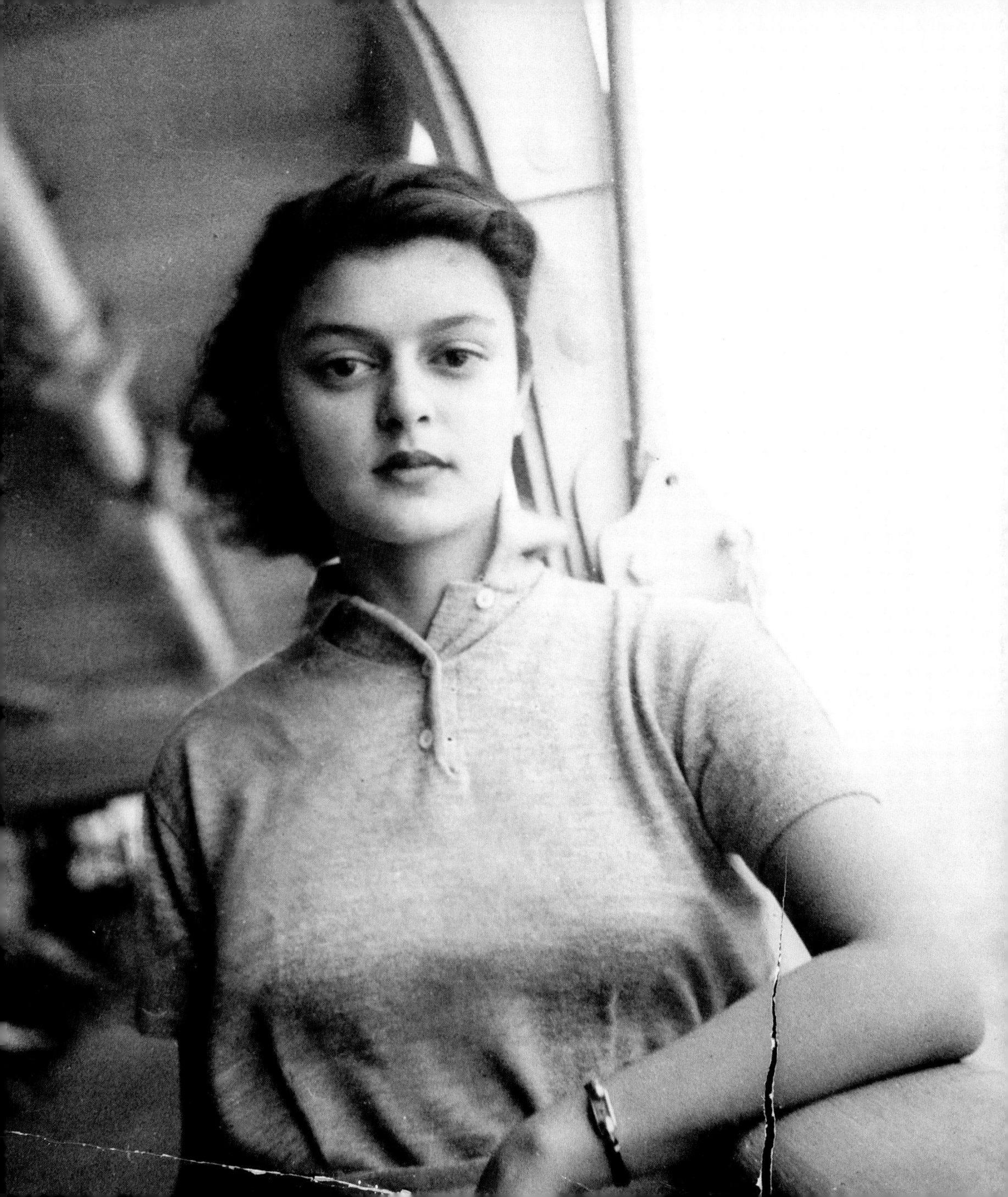

60 and 61 Donning stylish caps and hats came naturally to young Ayesha and she carried them off with her customary élan. Here she poses outside her house in Darjeeling on the left and in England (right) with her headgear.

62 and 63 Sport was an important element for the Cooch Behar children and they excelled in most of what they participated in. Ayesha was a good sportswoman and proficient in tennis, badminton and golf. Pictures on the left show her playing tennis and (on the right) enjoying a game of golf in Srinagar.

64 and 65 Ayesha was always game to try the different crafts that Jaipur offered. Here she cannot resist hav–
ing a go at the humble potter's wheel trying to make clay pots.

66 A hunting trip underway – elephants were the preferred mode of transportation when they had to go through the jungles of Cooch Behar looking for game.

66–67 Ooty offered many options for the sporty Ayesha who loved being outdoors. Here she is seen with friends waiting to row the boats onto the lake and (bottom) with a cousin.

68 top Ayesha and her cousin from Baroda Usha Raje Gaikwad pose for a photograph in a studio in London.

68 bottom and 68–69 Ramgarh lake located around 30 km from Jaipur was a very popular picnic spot where the family often took their guests boating and fishing.

70 and 70-71 Visits to Srinagar were full of recreational activities that included picnics in the company of friends and family. Leisurely time was spent cooking, playing games and relaxing in the beautiful countryside.

72 and 72-73 As far back as she can remember Ayesha always had several pets that she loved spending time with. As they had their own trains it was possible to take them along when they traveled out of Jaipur. Pictures show Ayesha with her pets in Ramgarh.

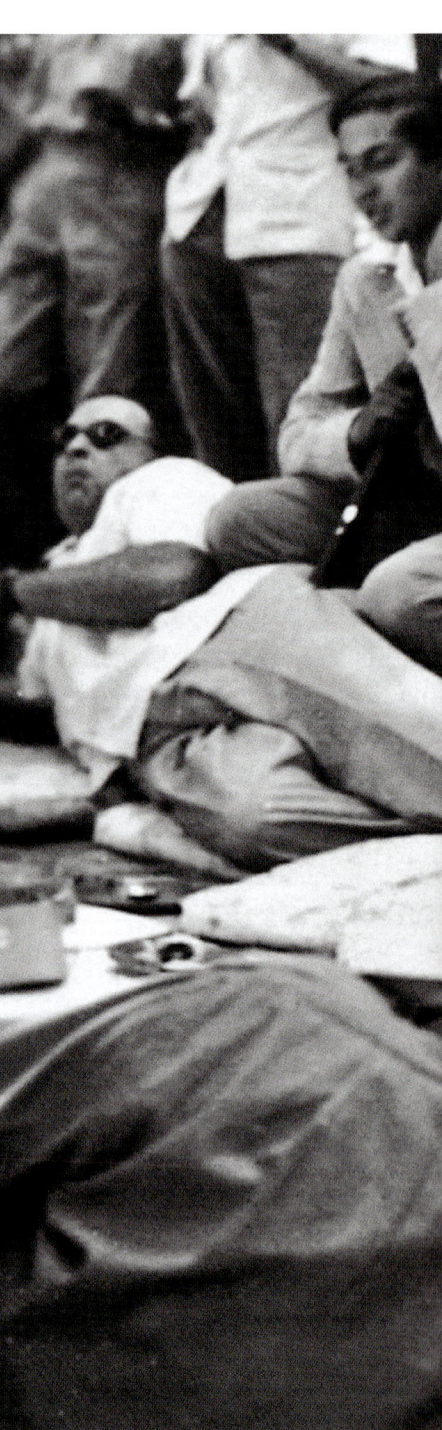

74 and 74–75 *Shikars* in Cooch Behar were not just about hunting but also meant spending time with their guests. Regardless of whether they managed to get their *shikar* or not they always had a lot of fun organizing their picnics.

76-77 Ayesha relaxing in her room in their Srinagar residence. Love for reading was a habit that was incul-
cated in her childhood years.

With Stars in Her Eyes

The finishing school was Ma Cooch Behar's plan to keep her daughter's mind occupied and, if possible, prevent her from falling in love. But it was all in vain because the four years that she had known the Maharaja of Jaipur had only made Gayatri Devi more determined than ever that she would indeed marry him. In 1936, Ma Cooch Behar took her family and left for Europe. Gayatri Devi's maternal grandmother took Ila and Maneka with her by boat and Ma Cooch Behar and Gayatri Devi followed them later by air.

Just before they left, the attention shifted, briefly, from Gayatri Devi to Ila Devi when Ma Cooch Behar heard that Ila Devi had secretly married a cousin of the Maharaja of Tripura, Romendra Kishore Dev Verma in a registry office in Calcutta. Ma Cooch Behar was both shocked and hurt by the fact that her daughter had been so defiant. She too had married against her parents' wishes but at least she had informed them and she could not reconcile herself to the fact that a princess could have married in so underhand and so undignified a manner. She decided to hold her peace and question Ila once she got to Paris. Gayatri Devi was relieved because she was free to dream about Jai.

When Ila Devi reached Paris there was a showdown and both mother and daughter had a lot of heated arguments but by the end the result was exactly what Ila had hoped for – a proper marriage befitting a princess would be arranged when they returned to India. This meant that the trousseau had to be put together so the first few weeks were spent in hectic shopping. From Paris they went on to London where the shopping continued.

Though quite involved in her older daughter's trousseau shopping, Ma Cooch Behar was equally attentive towards her younger daughter and not too happy with the fact that there were still four months before Gayatri Devi could go to her finishing school in Switzerland. Even in the midst of all the shopping and marriage plans Ma did not wish to let her waste time. When a friend suggested that Gayatri Devi be sent to a finishing school called the Monkey Club, for this brief period, Ma Cooch Behar liked the idea and enrolled the two younger girls there. What also helped her decision was the fact that they would be under the watchful eyes of their Baroda grandmother as well as a German Baroness.

"My mother was the one who recommended the Monkey Club to her," says friend Lady Kennard. "I was already enrolled there and since Ayesha and I had known each other earlier, we just continued spending a lot of time together." Lady Kennard, who is a niece of Lord Mountbatten, still visits Jaipur and is one of Gayatri Devi's few surviving school friends. "We had a wonderful time there. I do remember that she used to say that she would marry the Maharaja of Jaipur. When I said she couldn't because she would have to stay in *purdah* she said, 'No, I'm not going to be in *purdah*'."

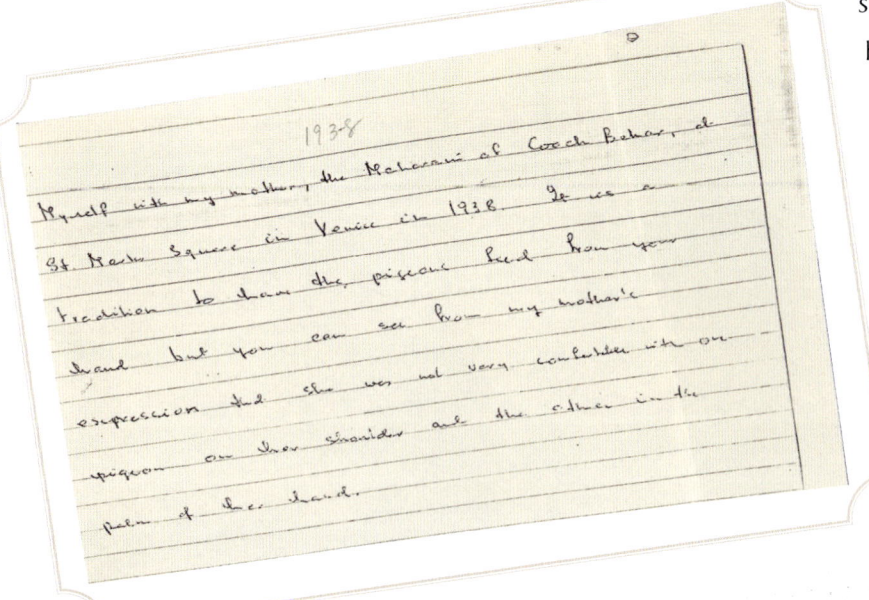

78 and 79 The family traveled extensively throughout Europe – Maharani Indira Devi and the young Ayesha in Venice in the 1930s.

80 and 81 Maharani Indira Devi was always escorted by one (sometimes all) of her children when she traveled to Europe. Here she is seen with Ayesha in Budapest and Spain and her son (bottom right) with another friend.

Waiting to Get Married

Both Jai and Gayatri Devi continued to meet regularly, and they spent as much time together as they could. This was possible because Indira Devi had to return to Cooch Behar so that she could organize a proper wedding for her older daughter Ila Devi. The younger two, Menaka Devi and Gayatri Devi, had stayed on in England with their grandmother and it was now easier for Gayatri Devi to sneak away to meet the dashing Maharaja. They went for drives, they went to restaurants and they were often seen at polo matches.

These regular meetings brought them closer and both now knew that they would like to spend their life together. When her stay at the Monkey Club came to a close and it was time to head towards Brillantmont in Lausanne, Gayatri Devi phoned Jai to bid him goodbye. Gayatri Devi had planned to take Menaka along with her but was persuaded by Jai to come alone as he wished to discuss something with

her. Gayatri Devi reached the lobby of the Dorchester Hotel and waited for Jai to pick her up from there. He arrived to take her for a drive around Hyde Park and said in a very matter of fact manner, "You know, I told Ma long ago that I'd like to marry you when you grow up." Gayatri Devi waited with bated breath for what followed. "You're only 16 now but I have to plan ahead for an event like that and make all sorts of arrangements, so I'd like to know if you want to marry me."

There was absolutely no hesitation, nor doubt in Gayatri Devi's mind and she agreed immediately to marry him. Maharaja Man Singh was a little disconcerted at this spontaneous and instant acquiescence and told her to take some time to think about it before giving her consent. But Gayatri Devi had never been more sure as she was then. She told Jai very confidently that she didn't want any time to think. She knew it was what she wanted.

82 and 83 When the Cooch Behars traveled to Srinagar they were often joined by the young Maharaja Man Singh of Jaipur. Since they were not yet married Man Singh visited Srinagar to spend time with Ayesha.

84 and 85 It was difficult for the young couple to stay away from each other and they looked for occasions when they could be together. Here the young Maharaja Man Singh spends time with his beloved Ayesha.

So even before she headed for Brillantmont, Gayatri Devi had taken perhaps the most important decision of her life. And if Ma Cooch Behar had hoped that being away at the finishing school would bring about a change of heart in her daughter it was not meant to happen. Gayatri Devi was now close to 17 and also old enough to know her own mind. While she perfected all the social graces and mannerisms befitting a princess, Gayatri Devi's love for Jai showed no signs of diminishing. Rajmata looks back on those heady days, "We were both young and very much in love. I thought it was the most romantic thing to have happened to me. Here was this handsome Maharaja from Jaipur who had so many admirers and yet he had chosen me."

After she was through with her time at the finishing school, she did not wish to return to India immediately so she was encouraged by Jai to join the London College of Secretaries. While the evenings were spent partying, the mornings were spent as 'Miss Devi' learning shorthand, typing, accounting, book keeping and so on. She had picked up a lot of useful skills

that she put into practice after her marriage. "I remember feeling a little embarrassed when I was asked what kind of job I was looking for. I really had no clue just how and where I would use the skills. However, what was good about those days was the fact that I could interact with normal people. Even after they learnt about me from newspapers, they were very matter of fact about it and took it in their stride as if having a princess learning typing in that college was an everyday event," says Rajmata.

Rajmata remembers it as one of the best times in her life: the phone calls and the elaborate plans to sneak out on dates without her chaperones getting any wiser made the courtship great fun for her because of the secrecy involved. "Altogether, it was a lovely and intoxicating time. We sealed it for ourselves by buying gold rings for each other with our names engraved inside." She was lucky that she had the support of Menaka and Indrajit who were confidantes and often ganged up with her to allow her more opportunity to spend time with Jai.

It did not matter in the least to Gayatri Devi that Maharaja Man Singh already had two wives. He was first married at the age of 12 to a princess of Jodhpur and then again, nine years later, to the first Maharani's niece. All she knew was that she was in love with him and wanted to spend the rest of her life with him.

While still in London, Gayatri Devi, on the insistence of Jai, wrote a letter to her mother informing her of her decision to marry him. After much resistance and reasoning with her daughter, Ma Cooch Behar had to give in and the young couple was engaged in 1939. Her only condition at that point was that they should wait for at least two years before getting married. "I think what troubled her most about this alliance was the fact that I would be the third wife. And she did not want Jai's second wife, of whom she had grown fond, to be hurt," says Rajmata of her mother's reluctance to give her approval to this match.

One of the main reasons that Ma Cooch Behar wanted the young couple to wait a few years before getting married was because she was still hoping that they would grow out of this attraction. More experienced in the ways of the world she did not think that it would be an easy life for her daughter and told her that she would be spending most of her married life in the nursery, looking after Jai's children. The other thing that troubled her was the matter of *purdah*. Ma Cooch Behar was very familiar with Rajasthan and knew that her daughter would have a difficult time coming to terms with the restrictions of the *zenana*, which still prevailed in Rajasthan.

Rajasthan in the 1940s was still a traditional, orthodox society where the activities of womenfolk were confined to their section of the residence. The *Zenana*, is a Persian term originating from *zan* or 'woman' under which a separate apartment is assigned to women family members and visitors to the family. More simply, female members interacted and relaxed in separate spaces within the family precinct. Ma Cooch Behar knew that her daughter would not be able to adjust in the *zenana* of the City Palace in Jaipur.

The heady days of England came to a temporary halt when Gayatri Devi returned to India. The first few months were spent in Bombay. Maharaja Man Singh was almost like a member of the family and continued to meet Gayatri Devi. Life was good, though a little restricted because she did not have the freedom that she had enjoyed in England where she could go unaccompanied to cinemas, plays and restaurants. Despite these restrictions there was enough opportunity for them to meet and spend time together. Ma Cooch Behar rented a house in Srinagar in 1939 and the entire family went off to spend summer there. They had a wonderful time and it was again a round of picnics, parties and more parties. The Cooch Behar boys were in great demand as was the handsome Maharaja Man Singh who managed to visit the Cooch Behars and spend some time with them. The three of them went together and were the life and soul of the parties that they attended. Menaka remembers those days, "You know, when Bhaiya, Indrajit and His Highness (Maharaja Man Singh) dressed up for formal parties in their uniforms and headgear they looked so handsome and impressive that we really felt very proud of them."

Towards the end of 1939, Maharaja Man Singh visited Calcutta during the polo season and met Ma Cooch Behar and requested that he be allowed to marry Gayatri Devi as soon as possible. World War II was just around the corner

and the menfolk had started moving back to their States, some to join their units and prepare to leave for the war front. This had changed things to a great extent and Maharaja Man Singh was keen to prepone his marriage. Ma Cooch Behar finally gave her approval and the young couple was officially engaged in March 1940, and the auspicious date that would make Gayatri Devi the third Maharani of Jaipur was set for April 17, 1940.

86 and 87 The royal couple Maharaja Man Singh and his bride Maharani Gayatri Devi were the toast of the town and a much sought after couple. No matter where they traveled they were the center of attraction.

THE THIRD MAHARANI
OF JAIPUR

1940-1950

The state of Jaipur was one of the more important principalities of the 22 princely states of Rajputana (the old name for Rajasthan) and accorded a 17-gun salute. Maharaja Sawai Man Singh was born as Mor Mukut Singh on August 21, 1911.

He was the second son of Thakur Sawai Singh of Isarda and his wife Sugan Kunwar, and his family was connected to the ruling house of Jaipur and Kota (where his father's sister was married). Maharaja Madho Singh II, the then Maharaja of Jaipur, did not have a legitimate heir to the throne of Jaipur though he had numerous children by various concubines. On March 24, 1921 Madho Singh II adopted the young Mor Mukut to be his son and heir. The boy was given the name 'Man Singh' upon his adoption. Madho Singh II died on September 7, 1922 and was succeeded by Man Singh as the next Maharaja of Jaipur and head of the Kachhwaha clan of Rajputs. The new Maharaja was merely 11 years old and one year after he was appointed the Maharaja, he was married to a princess from the Jodhpur family, a princely State that was similar to Jaipur in social ranking. This was a marriage that had been arranged by the elders of the family and he was duty bound to abide by it. His wife, Maharani Marudhar Kanwar, sister of Maharaja Sumer Singh of Jodhpur was 12 years his senior when they married in 1923. Eight years later Maharaja Man Singh went to Jodhpur again to marry his second wife, Maharani Kishore Kanwar, niece of his first wife and daughter of Sumer Singh. The first Maharani bore him two children – Princess Prem Kumari (Mickey) in 1929 and a son Bhawani Singh (Bubbles) in 1931. The second Maharani gave birth to two sons – Jai Singh (Joey) in 1933 and Prithviraj Singh (Pat) in 1935.

As the Maharaja of Jaipur, Man Singh took his duties very seriously and conducted the affairs of his state with great responsibility and foresight. He maintained good relations with his *Sardars*, or nobles, and brought about a radical improvement in his state forces. He created a new regiment, the Sawai Man Guards, that later went on to serve with distinction in World War II. Other than military affairs, Man Singh was a great polo enthusiast. He had the best polo team in the entire country with seven- and eight-handicap players while he himself was a nine-handicap player.

His passion for the sport led him to travel extensively at home and abroad. Perhaps the high point in his polo career came in 1933, when he took his team to London and stunned the polo world by demolishing almost all the polo teams and winning every single polo tournament that they participated in. This was one of the Jaipur team's most glorious moments and gave them a larger than life stature in the eyes of the western polo playing world.

88 There was something so ethereal about the beauty of Maharani Gayatri Devi of Jaipur that it inspired people to write poems in praise of her! A beautiful portrait.

91 The newly-wed Maharaja Sawai Man Singh of Jaipur poses with his glowing bride Maharani Gayatri Devi of Jaipur after their marriage in Cooch Behar in 1940.

92 Several artists painted the most striking portraits of the family. This beautiful portrait shows Jai (Maharaja Sawai Man Singh) in his formal dress complete with a turban and a *serpech*, or turban ornament.

94 These framed portraits of the rulers of Jaipur and Jodhpur still occupy pride of place in Rajmata's sitting room. The young Maharaja Sawai Man Singh of Jaipur is third from left in the bottom row.

95 An image of the attractively designed Jaipur coat of arms that was used by Maharaja Sawai Man Singh of Jaipur.

Man Singh was young, attractive and with his newly gained reputation as an extraordinarily talented and accomplished polo player he became the darling of the jet set in Europe. He was one of the best known of the young Maharajas of India and an idolized figure who was hero-worshipped by many among the younger set of royalty.

It was with this larger-than-life reputation behind him that Maharaja Man Singh walked into the life of the young Gayatri Devi, the princess of Cooch Behar, in the Thirties and just swept her off her feet. He created an everlasting impression on her and she was so enamored with him that she thought nothing of becoming his third wife toward the end of the decade.

After Ma Cooch Behar's consent the preparations for the wedding began in earnest. She set about ensuring that her daughter had a grand wed-

ding, befitting the princess of Cooch Behar. Maharaja Man Singh was understandably in a great hurry to take his bride with him to Jaipur. Gayatri Devi came down with diphtheria just before her marriage but Maharaja Man Singh refused to postpone the date any further and assured Ma Cooch Behar that the bride would be well looked after and given all possible time to complete her convalescence after marriage. Since the astrologers had suggested April 17 as an auspicious day he was determined to stick to that date. Unfortunately, just before the marriage there was a mishap, a tragic accident when Ma Cooch Behar's favorite brother Maharaj Dhairyashil of Baroda passed away. Now there was no choice but to postpone the marriage and the earliest date the astrologers could give was May 9.

His Highness
The Maharaja of Jaipur

96 and 97 Formal photographs of Jai taken on one of his frequent visits to London. These studio pictures were often used by painters to make huge portraits.

On May 9, 1940 Gayatri Devi finally wed her Prince Charming – just two weeks before her 21st birthday. Cooch Behar was a flutter of activity. The whole township seemed out to celebrate.

Though a lot of trousseau shopping had already been done in Europe and Ma Cooch Behar, given her great style, had ordered towels and sheets in Florence and Czechoslovakia, shoes and matching bags came from Salvatore Ferragamo in Florence, nightgowns in *mousseline de soie* from Paris, and the remainder of the shopping was done in Calcutta. Gayatri Devi set off for sari shopping and made a disastrous trip to a known shop and ordered saris in what she thought were appropriate colors. The poor

ary rituals being followed to ensure a long and happy married life to the royal couple. There was much jubilation when Man Singh reached the threshold and lightly touched the lintel in a customary gesture to announce his arrival as a bridegroom. The *puja* was long drawn out and both Maharaja Man Singh and Maharaj Kumari Gayatri Devi patiently went through the entire ceremony.

The marriage celebrations lasted for a full week and there were various lunches and dinners, music and dancing that continued for several days but both Maharaja Man Singh and Maharani Gayatri Devi stayed on in Cooch Behar for only for three days. When the marriage had been planned

shopkeeper, used only to Ma Cooch Behar's excellent taste, was shocked and immediately rang her up and asked her to come and see what her daughter had selected. As expected Ma Cooch Behar rejected all the saris and chided her daughter for her highly unacceptable choice. She changed her daughter's order and bought some 200 saris. Ma Cooch Behar's choice was impeccable and in the months to follow, Gayatri Devi, as the Maharani of Jaipur, was grateful that her mother had chosen the most appropriate clothing for her.

The great day finally dawned when on May 9, 1940 Maharaja Man Singh of Jaipur came to wed the princess of Cooch Behar in an impressive procession accompanied by 40 nobles from his State. The bridegroom was astride an elephant and the procession included several horses and dancing girls. The marriage ceremony was an elaborate one with their guests dressed in their traditional finery. Maharaja Man Singh was given a ceremonial welcome and cannons boomed to signal his entry through the gates of Cooch Behar palace. It was a traditional wedding with all the custom-

the young couple had decided to go to Ceylon (now Sri Lanka) for their honeymoon but had to change their plans due to the impending war. The next choice was Ooty, or Ootacamund, in south India.

She was now the Maharani of Jaipur and she got her first taste of what would follow in her new home. The *purdah* business started in Calcutta itself when the Jaipur Maharaja's staff just took over and kept all the male servants at bay. She was kept cloistered until the time she boarded the train. To her shock and discomfort her compartment was also covered with canvas screens on all sides so that no male member could set eyes on her. This was a new way of traveling and she was a little unnerved but decided it wasn't an appropriate time to tackle this issue. She would address it at a later stage.

For the young couple the time spent in Ooty was fun as they got to know each other more intimately and were able to spend time together without fear of being caught, which used to happen on their several clandestine dates. The days there were marked by hunts, picnics and parties

Our wedding ceremony in Cooch Behar
on the 19th May 1940.

98 and 99   Maharaja Sawai Man Singh (Jai) and Maharani Gayatri Devi (Ayesha) had a seven-year-long courtship before they were finally married. Pictures show the Maharaja as the bridegroom as he descends from an elephant in Cooch Behar; other pictures show the wedding ceremony in progress.

and informal get-togethers. Ooty being a popular summer destination, a lot of maharajas from other parts of the country were also there and Gayatri Devi tried to avoid the formal receptions for fear of offending the elder and more orthodox princes. It was still the 1940s and most of the maharajas present in Ooty were not used to their womenfolk participating in events that exposed them to the public eye.

The young couple did not let these little restrictions mar their one-month long honeymoon. It was full of merriment and Rajmata still treasures the hap-

py memories of that time. On May 23, 1940 Gayatri Devi celebrated her 21st birthday in Ooty and invited all the younger princes to her party. The fun and good times were interrupted briefly when Maharaja Man Singh had to leave for Bangalore to join his second wife and children. Maharani Gayatri Devi stayed behind in Ooty. She was to join him later as he'd told her to await his letter informing her when it was an appropriate time for her to come to Bangalore. When the letter came she

was just a little nervous because this would be her first meeting with the second Maharani Kishore Kanwar. She drove to Bangalore and as luck would have it Maharaja Man Singh was out of the house and her first meeting began on an awkward note. Fortunately for everybody there, Maharaja Man Singh arrived just then and managed to ease the tension and helped everybody behave and feel more normal. Very soon Maharani

Kishore became *Jo Didi* (older sister) because 'Jo' was what Maharaja Man Singh called her; it was short for Jodhpur, her home state.

This was also the time that Maharani Gayatri Devi got to spend more time with her husband's four children: Bubbles 9, Mickey 11 and the two younger boys, Joey 7 and Pat aged all of 5.

The Bangalore visit extended to two weeks and like their time in Ooty, was filled with parties, races and polo matches. All too soon it was time to leave for Jaipur. Maharani Gayatri Devi was just a little nervous because she had already had a taste of the stifling *purdah* and really wondered what her new home would be like? How would she tackle the *purdah* system? How would the other ladies greet her? These and other questions troubled her all the way on the train journey back to Jaipur. "Jai understood my nervousness and tried to reassure me as best as he could but I couldn't help being quite anxious much as I tried to control my feelings," Rajmata recalls.

This was her first trip to Jaipur as the Maharani of Jaipur; her earlier trips had been very informal with hardly any protocol, but this trip was different. When the royal saloon approached Jaipur, Maharaja Man Singh gently told Gayatri Devi to be prepared to get into traditional clothes. Viman Bhawan, their personal waiting rooms at the railway station, were decorated with flowers and festoons to welcome the newly married Maharaja

100 It is easy to see the glow of happiness on the faces of the newly-weds. The wedding was followed by several days of formal functions in which the royal couple had to participate.

101 One of the first formal portraits of the royal couple soon after their marriage. Maharaja Sawai Man Singh is in his army uniform and below a slightly more informal portrait of the royal couple.

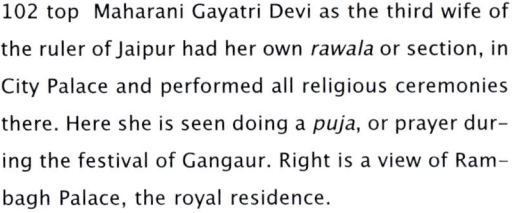

102 top Maharani Gayatri Devi as the third wife of the ruler of Jaipur had her own *rawala* or section, in City Palace and performed all religious ceremonies there. Here she is seen doing a *puja*, or prayer during the festival of Gangaur. Right is a view of Rambagh Palace, the royal residence.

102 bottom Maharaja Man Singh already had four children when he married Maharani Gayatri Devi. Seen in this picture left are Joey (Maharaj Jai Singh), Mickey (Maharaj Kumari Prem Kanwar) and Bubbles (Maharaj Kumar Bhawani Singh). Bottom right: the three brothers - nine-year-old Bubbles (Maharaj Kumar Bhawani Singh), seven-year-old Joey (Maharaj Jai Singh) and five-year-old Pat (Maharaj Kumar Prithviraj Singh).

and his new Maharani. The comfortably furnished suite of rooms was designed with two separate wings for the maharaja and maharani and their important guests so that they could change and freshen up prior to appearing before the public. It was also more convenient for the visiting dignitaries to board the train away from the crowded public station.

When the train rolled into the station, Gayatri Devi was relieved to see her maids from Cooch Behar waiting for her with the appropriate clothes that she had to wear before the people of Jaipur were allowed even a glimpse of her. The maids of the second Maharani, Jo *Didi* were also present at the station to help her. She was whisked away to change into a dressy *paushak*, the *lehanga* (long skirt*)*, *kurti kanchli* (two piece blouse*)* and *odhna* (sari), traditional clothes that she was expected to

wear. Rajmata remembers the clothes she wore on that day, "As a new bride I had to wear a bright red *paushak* with all the traditional jewelry. The only item of traditional jewelry where I cheated a bit was with the *nath*, or nose ring; my nose was not pierced so my mother had arranged a clip-on one for me."

When she had donned her heavily sequinned *paushak*, she left her suite to be formally welcomed by Maharaja Man Singh's two married sisters and a number of other ladies, just outside Viman Bhawan. They escorted her to nearby Amber where the fort houses the temple of Goddess Shila Devi, the Jaipur family shrine. It was a ritual with Maharaja Man Singh – he visited the family shrine to offer prayers before leaving town as well as upon his return.

103 This family portrait was taken in Rambagh when Ayesha's mother Maharani Indira Devi of Cooch Behar visited Jaipur with her mother Maharani Chimnabai of Baroda. Also seen in the photograph are the Jaipur children and other guests.

From Amber they headed towards Rambagh Palace which was to be Maharani Gayatri Devi's new home. Set amongst beautiful gardens with plenty of trees, Gayatri Devi was relieved to see the lush greenery surrounding the palace that was reminiscent of her home in Cooch Behar. Rambagh, though thoroughly modern in its design and planning, was built to follow the traditional pattern of separate wings for the Maharaja – the *mardana* and the Maharani – the *zenana*. Maharani Gayatri Devi's wing had been modernized by Maharaja Man Singh and she was delighted to find her apartments done to suite her taste. "His Highness had the rooms specially redecorated for me by his favorite interior designer, Hammonds of London. The rooms had pale cream fitted carpets, light pink walls, a beautiful chandelier and pale pink brocade curtains embellishing the wide win-

dows. My bedroom was the prettiest in the palace, furnished with a bed of soft silk satin with light brocade bedspreads, a colorful divan, two armchairs with silver legs and a mirrored dressing table trimmed with pleated silk satin," Rajmata recalls.

The first 10 days after her arrival in Jaipur were a succession of religious ceremonies and formal get-togethers where she met all the relatives and close friends of Maharaja Man Singh, but life soon fell into a pattern. "Every morning we used to go riding and swimming. I did observe *purdah* when I went for the formal *grihapravesh* (formal entry into the house) ceremony at City Palace and on other formal occasions. But His Highness never used to say that I can't go out, I can't do this, I can't do that," says Rajmata.

104 and 105 A little known fact about the Maharani of Jaipur is that she happily spent some time as an army officer's wife when Maharaja Man Singh joined the Indian Army in September 1940. He was posted to Risalpur and joined the 13th Lancers. Here she is seen in Jaipur inspecting the Rajendra Hazari Guards in Jaipur.

Her formal visit to City Palace was on a day declared auspicious by the pundits and she still remembers it very clearly. "When we reached the outer gates of City Palace, I was transferred into a palanquin and carried through a labyrinth of corridors and courtyards. Then I was set down and as a new bride, had to perform a prayer ceremony at the threshold to mark my entry into my husband's home." She recalls the other customs equally well, "After this there was a woman's *darbar*, when one by one the ladies of the *zenana* and of the aristocratic families filed past me, parting my veil to look at my face and leaving a gift on my lap after their first glimpse of me." Since the *zenana* was made up of several self-contained

The easy informality and the western lifestyle of Cooch Behar were replaced by the formal and traditional state of affairs and a lot of things seemed different here. Obviously, life in Jaipur was certainly not the kind she was accustomed to but she wasn't complaining. However, what hadn't really changed were the parties, picnics, *shikars* and the constant stream of visitors who added a lot of excitement to their early years. Unlike the other two older Maharanis who spent most of their time in their section of the palace, Maharani Gayatri Devi was the perfect hostess, entertaining her guests and mixing with them with ease.

The staid and proper city was used to its womenfolk being in *purdah* and the only job expected of them was the smooth running of the house and care of their children. The new Maharani was something of a novelty and not everyone was happy to welcome this modern Maharani who moved around freely and accompanied the Maharaja to parties. There was resistance from most of the orthodox nobles who didn't quite know how to handle the new and 'shocking' state of affairs.

apartments she too got her own section which was decorated in blues and greens with a courtyard and a large room for her own private functions. She loved her section and was to have many formal functions there in the years to come.

City Palace fascinated the new Maharani by the sheer beauty of its Rajput architecture. Each section of this 18th century sprawling palace was breathtakingly beautiful. The courtyards, the carved lattices, the marble pillars and facades, the painted doorways and chambers were totally different from her palace in Cooch Behar and she loved the exquisite craftsmanship that had gone into its planning. She also went to offer prayers at the family shrine of Govind Devji that stood to the north of the Palace.

For the Maharani, however these were minor problems and she quickly put them behind her. There was so much to do that life became more and more interesting as the days progressed. Surrounded as she was by ladies in *purdah* who had to be almost forced to leave their homes she was determined to draw these orthodox Rajput women out of *purdah*.

106 and 107 The Thakur of Dudu was closely associated with the Jaipur family as he was the Jaipur Maharani's election officer, and his village, located 65 km to the west of Jaipur, was a popular spot for duck shooting. Pictures show one such visit to Dudu.

In 1942, just two years after her marriage, the Maharani was to come up with the most revolutionary idea of her life, an idea that would impact the lives of countless women in the next few years. She decided to set up a school for the Rajput women. To the well-educated Maharani this seemed the best way of achieving her objective. Fortunately, Maharaja Man Singh supported her in her revolutionary ideas and set up a team to assist her. The team had the best thinkers of the state and was comprised of Pandit Amarnath Atal, the Finance Minister; Sir Mirza Ismail, the Dewan of Jaipur State; Savitri Bharatiya, the Inspectress of Schools and a few other progressive people. Very soon a suitable building, Madho Vilas, was identified. The biggest hurdle of all came in persuading the *thikanedars*, or nobility, to send their girls to this school. It was a royal command and nobody dare defy it. Most of the nobles decided that it would be easier to go along with the idea rather than oppose it and most hoped that it was one of those passing fancies that would die a natural death.

The new school was named after her – Maharani Gayatri Devi Girls Public School and opened its doors to students of all ages on August 12, 1943. "You want to know why I considered education so important?" asks Rajmata. "You see, I was fortunate enough to receive a sound education and had very enlightened, strong women on my father's as well as my mother's side of the family. I realized that if I wanted to draw Rajput women out of *purdah* then I would have to do a lot more than organize tournaments, raffles and parties at the Ladies Club. Fortunately His Highness agreed with me and I was able to start the Maharani Gayatri Devi Girls School."

The prospectus of the school in 1943 said: *"The aims of the institution will be…To secure to the pupils the advantages of training in home craft and domestic hygiene, for the betterment and happiness of their homes…to create in them, a taste for fine arts, colour decoration and culture…to create, through games, good physique and esprit-de-corps in the girls. In general, the aim and effort would be, to impart an all round education to the girls, which will prepare them to play the role required of them, as efficient members of the society."*

The school provided a sound education to countless young girls from Jaipur as well as other parts of the country. It soon gained a reputation as one of the most prestigious schools of its time. Students came from diverse backgrounds. An old student of MGD School (she joined the school in 1948) remembers those early days, "We joined the school because our parents were literally ordered to send us to this new school started by the Maharani Sahiba of Jaipur. We were all new to this concept and there was no such thing as regular classes. We did a little of everything including dancing and singing! We were more enamored of our founder. She was a cult figure. We used to gaze at her with such great admiration and we used to try and copy her hairstyle…she has this habit of flicking her hair, you know, so we used to stand in front of the mirror for hours and practice it!"

Maharani Gayatri Devi led by example: she wore trousers, drove her own car, played tennis, golf and badminton and went horseback riding. For her there was never a dull moment. She revived the activities of the Ladies Club, and being a good badminton player she soon went on to become the President of the Badminton Association of India as well as the Vice President of the National Tennis Association. She enjoyed her game of tennis but ended up playing mainly with male partners because hardly any women could play the game. Gradually, some of the *thikana* ladies who regularly went to the City Palace brought about a change in their own lifestyles just to be able to keep pace with the new and revolutionary Maharani. Within a very short period she had become an icon, a role model for women throughout the country. She was the original *Bold and Beautiful* woman of her time.

108 As the Maharani of Jaipur, Ayesha always made time for young students and encouraged them to participate in varied activities.

109 Soon after their marriage Jai took his new bride to Bangalore and spent time there. Here he poses with her and his car outside their home in Bangalore. Bottom: a copy of Ayesha's first driving license that was made in the name of Maharaj Kumari Gayatri Devi of Cooch Behar, resident of Woodlands, Alipore, Calcutta. The license dates back to December 19, 1940.

110 Polo took the Jaipur family all over the world. After polo there was always time to meet and spend time with friends.

111 During one of their trips to the west Ayesha, Bubbles and a cousin witnessed a film shooting with Hollywood actress Vivien Leigh.

112–113 When Jai played polo in England, Ayesha almost always accompanied him. Here she is seen relaxing with a friend as they watch a game of polo in England.

114 and 115 As the Maharani of Jaipur, Ayesha had to be formally dressed most of the time
but that did not stop her from participating in sporting activities. In these photographs, taken
in Ooty, Ayesha is playing table tennis with her sari tucked at her waist.

116 top and 116–117 Swimming was an outdoor activity that was enjoyed by Ayesha and Jai and they were always keen to try and get a good swim whenever possible. Pictures show Ayesha with her brother and friends in Srinagar and England.

116 bottom A lot of royal States of India had their own cricket teams where they often played friendly matches against each other. This picture was taken during a cricket match in Jaipur.

118 and 118–119 Ranthambhore continues to hold a special place in Ayesha's heart and it's a place she likes to visit every year. She has fond memories of countless *shikar* trips that she made with her friends and family.

THE TATLER AND BYSTANDER
LONDON
JULY 23, 1917

THE
TATLER
and BYSTANDER

One Shilling and Sixpence
Vol. CLXXXV. No. 2402

HER HIGHNESS THE MAHARANI OF JAIPUR

120   The stylishly elegant Maharani of Jaipur alights from an airplane on one of her several trips out of the country.

121 top   The Maharaja and Maharani of Jaipur were invited all over the world and were hosted by heads of state across the globe. Picture on top shows the royal guests being escorted around on one such tour.

121 bottom   This was the period when Maharani Gayatri Devi of Jaipur was written about in all major international magazines and newspapers. Picture shows her on the cover of Tatler magazine.

Her list of admirers grew and people showered her with praise. A senior diplomat says, "You know, she [Rajmata] doesn't realize it but she was a revolutionary. She was an educationist who started this school for girls and made it possible for women all over Rajasthan to come out of *purdah*. She was the first woman to attend a public function in Udaipur in 1952 and I can tell you it caused quite a stir."

She was like a dream come true and people who have seen her in her earlier days are still at a loss for words when they try to describe her beauty. Indira Atal, from the family of Raja Amar Nath Atal, the education Minister of Jaipur State – now in her 70s –, first saw the young Maharani at Mumbai airport a few years after her marriage. "I'm a Bombay person, quite blasé about things. I'd seen a lot of film stars and other glamorous people and wasn't easily impressed. Yet I still remember the first time I saw the Maharani. My husband told me to look towards the plane – and there she was! She was wearing a blue shirt and trousers and was walking down the steps. Oh my god, I'd never seen anybody so beautiful in my life. She was out of this world, really, the most gorgeous woman I'd ever seen."

More and more people who met her or saw her pictures were also absolutely enamored of her persona. In her book, *Beauty and Health*, the 'Grande Dame of Romance', the late Barbara Cartland noted: *"Ayesha Jaipur has been called the loveliest woman in the world. She is, when one sees her, breathtakingly beautiful with that fascinating feminine grace which is characteristic of Indian women. She has also an excellent brain and a capacity for hard work. She has for ten years represented Jaipur in Parliament. Jaipur with its pink palaces full of incredible treasures, tiger-infested green hills, marble rocks and atmosphere of mystery, is a fitting background for someone so exquisite that a poet wrote of her: "Her face is lovelier than the golden light; Which brings the Indian dawn." Ayesha Jaipur has friends over the whole world, from the poor families she represents in India who look on her as their champion and protector, to the Royal and social figures of the West. She inspires them all with love, loyalty and trust. She has a deep compassion for suffering, but also a strong desire to do something to help. She is one of those rare people of whom one can truthfully say: "Her eyes mirror her soul."*

When she wasn't busy looking into the smooth running of the school the new Maharani was entertaining guests. There was a separate wing for the various guests, including several Maharajas and polo players who visited during the polo season; they were a constant feature at the Rambagh. And entertaining their guests was a serious business for the royal families. If there were insufficient rooms for them, as very often there were extra guests who had to be accommodated, neat and comfortable tent camps were often put up on the lawns to take care of this problem.

123 A photograph of Maharani Gayatri Devi taken in a studio in London in the late Forties.

124 and 125   The late Fifties and early Sixties saw even greater recognition for Maharani Gayatri Devi of Jaipur and she came to be listed among the 10 most beautiful women in the world.
Here the beautiful Maharani is seen in three different poses.

This idyllic life was interrupted several times in the early Forties. The first Maharani Marudhar Kanwar died in 1944 at the age of 45, due to liver failure; then the continuing war in Europe also impacted as the palace activities had to be curtailed. Closer to home, India's freedom struggle had also reached its crescendo. In 1947, India finally achieved the Independence for which the country had struggled for all these years and the political upheaval continued. This was also the time of the partition of the country with the formation of Pakistan. This led to widespread bloodshed and many parts of the country grappled with communal riots. Thousands were killed in the violence that spread throughout the country. Jaipur fortunately did not see too much of it and the Maharaja played a major role

employed political negotiations backed with the option of military action to ensure the primacy of the Central government and of the Constitution then being drafted.

Things changed rapidly after that. There were a lot of changes that were forced on the maharajas all over the country. The political atmosphere was not very conducive and the ruling princes were left to negotiate individually for a better deal. Jaipur was no different. It was integrated into the new Union of Greater Rajasthan. In doing so Maharaja Man Singh not only handed over all the money in his treasury to the Government but all official buildings were also transferred to the State Government in 1949. The property that changed hands was worth over 15 million pounds in those days.

in maintaining law and order when he patrolled the streets in an open jeep to ensure that there was no violence in the city. For him all the citizens of his state were alike and he considered all the people as his children whether they were Hindus or Muslims. It was thanks to this that Jaipur did not see any instances of communal riots.

British India at that time consisted of 562 princely states and though the princes of these states initially had the right to remain independent or join either nation, the merger of the states was a foregone conclusion. None of new India's leaders were willing to face the prospect of a nation fragmented into medieval-era kingdoms. The new Government of India

Four months after Independence, Maharaja Man Singh had what was to be the last grand function as the Maharaja of Jaipur. In December he celebrated his Silver Jubilee as the ruler of Jaipur. It was a spectacular affair attended by ruling princes from neighboring states and friends from overseas. The culmination of the festivities was a majestic *darbar* that was attended by the Viceroy to India, and the Jaipur family's personal friend, Lord Mountbatten who came with his wife.

After the silver jubilee celebrations were over and their guests had all been seen off, the Maharaja and Maharani made a quick trip to Cooch Behar to be with Bhaiya to celebrate *his* silver jubilee.

126 In 1947 Maharaja Man Singh celebrated his silver jubilee and was visited by many of his friends to join him in the celebrations. Pictures on the left show Lord and lady Mountbatten being welcomed by Jai and Ayesha.

127 There was a special ceremony held in the Darbar Hall of City Palace, the home of Maharaja Man Singh that was attended by all the nobles of the Jaipur State. Picture shows the Maharaja in the *darbar* and (bottom) on his way to the City Palace.

128 The Silver Jubilee function included a plethora of varied activities that included the Maharaja of Jaipur being weighed in silver coins that were later distributed to the poor.

129 top For Maharaja Man Singh it was a time of hectic activity that also saw him doing *puja*, a religious ceremony, during his Silver Jubilee celebrations.

129 bottom A guest being received in a traditional manner for a function in the Palace.

Earlier in 1948 there was another display of princely grandeur. Princess Prem Kumari – Mickey – was married to the Maharaja of Baria's eldest son. Rajmata recalls that marriage, "She was the first Jaipur princess to be married in a hundred years. The wedding and the attendant processions, banquet and celebrations were on a scale of unparalleled lavishness. It was perhaps the final grand display of the pageantry of princely India." The famous photographer Henri Cartier-Bresson came to take the pictures and this marriage was later mentioned in *The Guinness Book of World Records* as the most expensive wedding in the world.

After this marriage both Maharaja Man Singh and Gayatri Devi went to the United States, a country they hadn't visited before, and enjoyed their stay there. On their return Maharaja Man Singh got involved with the process of integration of the princely states and was there to push for Jaipur's role in the new scheme of things. This year marked the end of an era when on January 30, 1948 Mahatma Gandhi was assassinated in Delhi, and there was much chaos and confusion which took all of the Indian Government's tact and skill to control.

As a mark of respect and also to acknowledge Maharaja Man Singh's role in the smooth integration of the princely states he was made the Rajpramukh (Governor) in March 1949. Man Singh threw himself into his duty to his people and was fairly happy with whatever he had. He noted: *"I feel happy and proud that I find no change in my people's love, affection and loyalty towards me and I had a rousing reception from all sects of my people wherever I went and met them at most functions."*

130 and 131 Jai had four children before he married Ayesha – three sons and one daughter. Jagat, his fourth son, was born on October 15, 1949. Picture shows the proud parents with their newborn.

On 15th October 1949, Maharani Gayatri Devi gave birth to her only son Maharaj Kumar Jagat Singh. She had moved to Bombay during the time of his birth and stayed on there for a month. She recalls the festivities when news of Maharaja Man Singh's fourth son reached Jaipur. It was no longer a princely State but the Chief Minister of Rajasthan happily declared a public holiday and cannons were fired to commemorate the birth of the baby boy. Crowds gathered at Rambagh to congratulate the Maharaja and likened him to King Dashratha of the epic Ramayana who also had four sons."

Things were changing and changing very rapidly. "There was a gradual erosion of our way of life and weakening of our identity with our state – and indeed, the identity of the state itself," noted Rajmata in her memoirs.

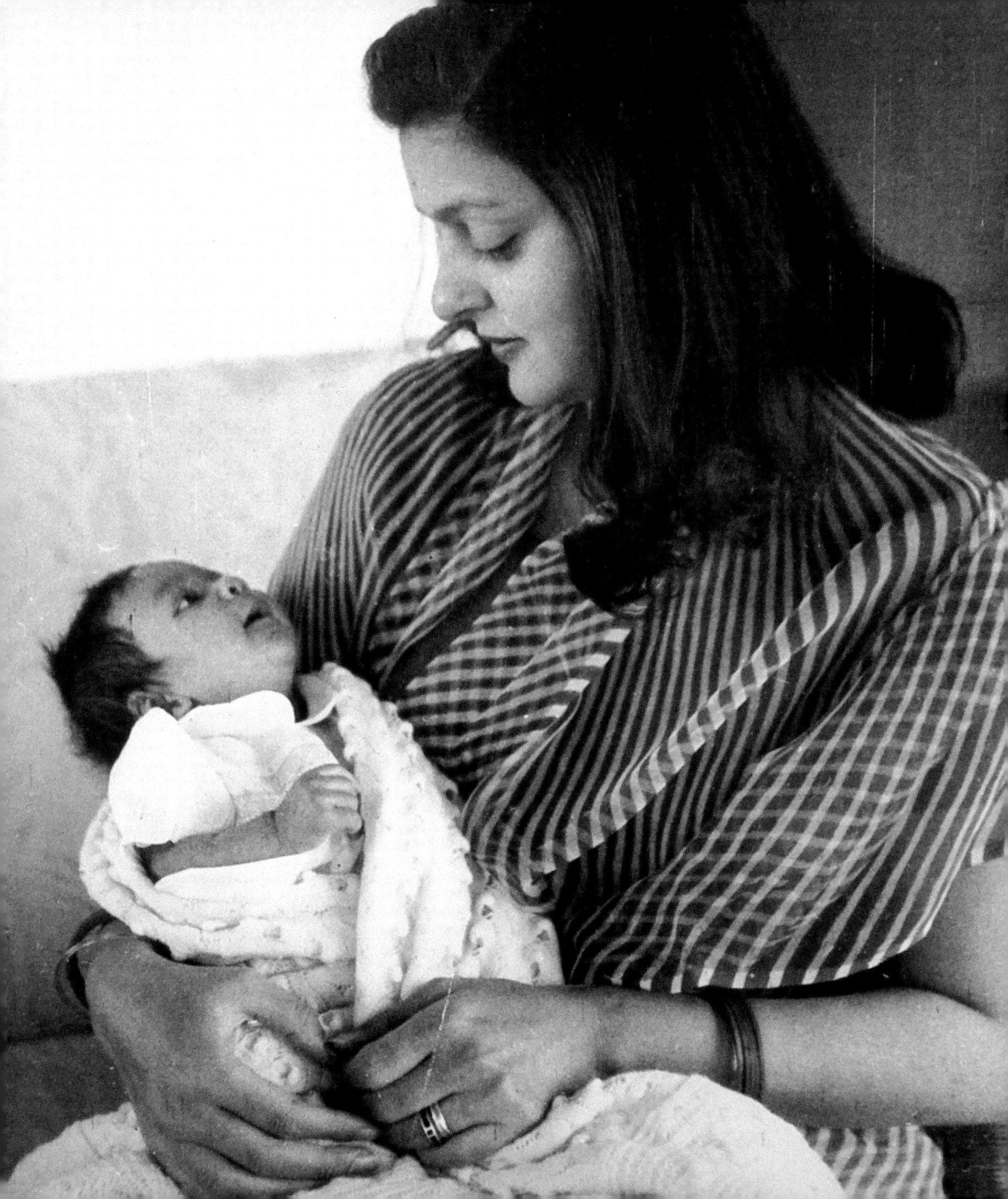

A CHARMED LIFE IN JAIPUR

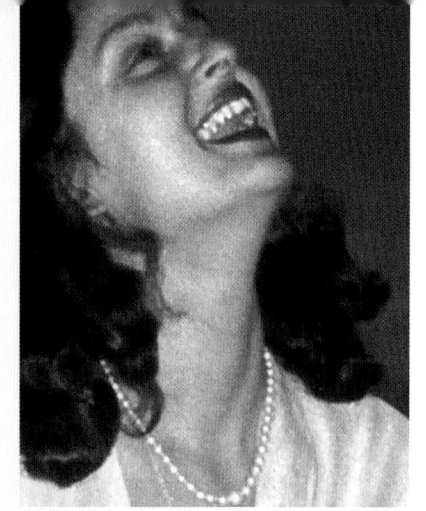

1950-1960

Maharaja Man Singh's life was divided between England and India. Polo was a passion for him and he began putting his team together when he returned from England in the 1930s. The Jaipur polo team astounded the world with their performances and won every major polo championship.

Polo, Parties, Picnics and More

On January 26, 1950 India became a republic and a new constitution came into effect. Changes were inevitable and an ongoing process for the Indian Government. The ruling princes found themselves a part of this change yet did not really have an important role to play unless they were given a responsible post, as Jaipur had been given. They tried to cope with the situation as best as they could. The chamber of princes that had been established in 1921 was meant to provide a forum in which princes could interact with the Government and discuss their problems and the Government's policies that impacted their lives.

In Jaipur for a while, life seemed to fall into the old pattern and a major part of the year was devoted to sporting activities more than anything else. A lot had changed, but what did not change was Maharaja Man Singh's first love – polo – to which he turned his attention.

He travelled to Europe and kept away from politics as much as he could. The Argentine team arrived in Jaipur to play polo and stayed on for three months during which time there were polo matches, parties and a lot of traveling between Bombay, Delhi and Jaipur where the teams moved for their tournaments.

The children were now in various stages of their education. The three boys, Bubbles, Joey and Pat, were in Harrow and it was more convenient to have a permanent base in England. Maharaja Man Singh bought an estate in West Sussex called Saint Hill, then in Berkshire and a flat in Grosvenor Square in London.

Tragedy struck in 1951 when Gayatri Devi's brother Indrajit died in a tragic mishap at the age of 33. Battling with a drinking problem he was undergoing treatment when he went off to Darjeeling. There he accidentally dropped a cigarette on his blankets and set them ablaze. Gayatri Devi was shattered by this tragic incident and wished that she could spend more time with her mother who was now more or less on her own, but her life was now in Jaipur and there were duties that she had to fulfill as the Maharani of Jaipur. This was also a period when a succession of important guests arrived in Jaipur. Among them were the Mountbattens, the Russian President Khrushchev, Bulganin, Jackie Kennedy, Eleanor Roosevelt and Queen Elizabeth. Arrangements had to be made for each of them and official entertainment meant a lot of meticulous planning.

132 The incredibly beautiful mother and her equally good-looking son. Maharani Gayatri Devi poses for a photograph with the young Maharaj Kumar Jagat Singh in a studio in London.

135 and 136 Life for Maharaja Man Singh seemed to revolve around his passion for polo. He excelled in the game and was happiest when astride a horse playing with his team. Pictures show him and Ayesha with the victor's trophy.

137 After a polo game in Deauville, Maharaja Man Singh and his team won the Gold Cup in 1957; a proud Ayesha holds the trophy and Jai's polo hat.

In Deauville 1958 — the proud wife carrying her husband's trophy + polo helmet. Our son Jagat looks equally pleased.

138 and 138–139 When Jai played polo he had Ayesha and other members of the family as avid spectators. (Right) Jai and Ayesha watch a game in progress with other dignitaries.

140 There were many occasions when the winner's trophy was handed over to Jai by his wife Ayesha! Bottom is a line-up of the two polo teams after the match.

141 top and bottom Maharaja Man Singh being felicitated by the President of India – Dr Rajendra Prasad (bottom); Maharaja Man Singh being felicitated yet again for a winning performance (top).

141 center It absolutely delighted the spectators to watch this little drama on the polo ground when the Maharani of Jaipur handed over the prize to her husband – the Maharaja of Jaipur.

142 top The Maharani of Jaipur arrives to watch a game of polo.

142 bottom Young Bubbles – Maharaj Kumar Bhawani Singh, a proficient polo player himself – joins Maharani Gayatri Devi to watch a polo game.

142–143 Polo was more than just a game – it was a social event where the players, their wives and friends gathered to watch and join in the festivities after the game. Picture shows Maharani Gayatri Devi waiting for the prizes to be placed on the table behind her.

Calcutta Races. 1st January, 1958. The Metropolitan. 6 Fur. H. H. The Maharaja of Cooch Behar's "A M A P A" 7-10 Stirk up. Time:- 1 Minute 11-4/5 seconds. Trained by Mr.Sibbritt.

144 top At the Calcutta racecourse with her brother, the Maharaja of Cooch Behar. Their stay in Calcutta was marked by regular trips to the racecourse there.

144 bottom Maharani Gayatri Devi was a common sight on polo fields and racecourses and was a very good rider herself.

145 Maharani Gayatri Devi's love for horses continues to this day and she visits her stables everyday to feed and check on her horses. Picture shows her feeding her favorite horse.

Capt. Raghubir Singh of Dundlod, Self, Bulganin, H.H. Khrushchev their aide at the City Palace on the occasion of a Banquet in the Russian honour. Study of attention for their children.

146 and 147 Among the many dignitaries who visited Jaipur were Marshal Bulganin and Nikita Krushchev. They are seen here with Maharaja Man Singh and Maharani Gayatri Devi at the City Palace. The Jaipur royals also visited Russia on their invitation and did a lot of sightseeing while there. Pictures show them at the Red Square in Moscow.

148 and 149 By the early Fifties Maharaja Man Singh had bought Saint Hill Manor, East Grinstead in West Sussex and the family took to spending their summers there. They entertained often and also went off for vacations with friends. Pictures show Jai and Ayesha spending some happy times in England and the South of France.

It was not just official entertainment as the Maharani loved to throw informal parties and tried to do something different each time. There were cooking parties, picnics, fancy dress parties and 'ghost' parties. People who attended these parties remember them with fondness. Her sense of humor and her love for playing practical jokes on her guests was an endearing aspect of her nature. Maharaja Man Singh's sister, Chand Baisa recalls an incident that took place during the late Fifties. "One day we were getting bored so Maharani Saheb (Rajmata) decided to visit some friends. She asked me to accompany her and I happily agreed until I realized that she wanted to go in a bullock cart! I was horrified because I knew that His Highness would not approve and would certainly get annoyed with me for allowing her to do so. I tried my best to dissuade her but she can be quite stubborn. Can you imagine, here we were, the two of us, and we climbed onto some poor man's covered bullock cart that was carrying hay. When the man realized who his passengers were he was too scared to protest and nervously took us to this house and went right up to the porch. The lady of the house came out

shouting and abusing the poor man for bringing the cart into the house without permission. The poor man could only mumble that the 'passengers' had forced him to come here. Unable to control her laughter anymore, Maharani Sahib coolly jumped down from the cart. After the lady recovered from her shock she begged the Maharani not to play such pranks again otherwise His Highness would throw *them* out of the State! She was so full of fun and games that there was never a dull moment when she was around."

There was also a famous 'skeleton party' that is remembered to this day. One day Maharani Gayatri Devi decided to have a skeleton party party and sought the approval of the senior Maharani who said, "My happiness is in seeing you all happy so you do what you want to do." A dinner was organised at Lily Pool (her present residence) and a volunteer was made to wear black clothes with a skeleton drawn on it. The entire garden area would be in darkness and just the area where the skeleton was to be lowered would be lit up, just enough to see the skeleton. The idea was to see how many people would get scared and

150 and 151 Jai and Ayesha were much sought-after guests during their trips abroad and Jai's added responsibility as the Indian Ambassador to Spain saw him traveling across Europe and meeting people from all walks of life. There were parties and meetings that the popular couple attended as part of their duty. Though royal duties kept them busy most of the time the Jaipurs also made time to meet and party with their friends who visited them from all over the world. Maharani Gayatri Devi was well-known for her informal and interesting parties and picnics.

how many were really brave. When the party was in full swing the skeleton was suddenly lowered and there was chaos because most of the guests were so scared that they didn't even stay long enough to have their dinner!

Devika Devi, daughter of the Maharani's elder sister Ila Devi also remembers some fun times that she witnessed when she was in Jaipur to visit her aunt. She fooled her cousin Gautam Narayan when he came to Jaipur to visit her. "Gautam Narayan was very simple. He said everybody talks so highly of Jo *Didi* I would like to meet her and pay my respects to her. He had never seen her before. So *Masi Ma* (Rajmata) said of course you must meet her. Then she got this brilliant idea of dressing up one of the senior maids to look like Her Highness (Jo *Didi*). She warned Gautam Dada that Jo *Didi* did not speak very good English so he would have to converse with her in Hindi. She even coached him as to how he must greet her and what he should say to her. Everything was arranged and everybody, including Jo *Didi*, hid behind the thick curtains and waited for the drama to unfold. The poor maid was nervous

but she was quite used to these pranks so she sat on the sofa and waited to receive Gautam Dada. I was made to sit next to the maid to make the scene look more authentic. The poor man came in and greeted her respectfully. The maid couldn't speak a word of English so she just sat there nervously and nodded her head. Finally gathering her wits about her she mumbled, '*Kumar kaise hain aap*' ('Kumar, how are you?') Gautam Dada also looked on nervously and wondered how to keep the conversation going. Suddenly, another cousin who was hiding behind the curtain couldn't hold his laughter anymore and poked his head out. Gautam Dada realized that there was something funny going on. Then *Masi Ma* came out from her hiding place and said, 'Now, I'll introduce you to the real Maharani'. Incidentally, Jo *Didi* spoke excellent English. The game up, all of us thoroughly enjoyed ourselves. She really kept everybody on their toes with her practical jokes."

Practical jokes and the resultant fun and laughter were normal in the *zenana*, and something that provided the bored ladies with some enjoyable activity when they found themselves at a loose end. But *zenanas*

152 and 153 People remember the parties that Ayesha as the Maharani of Jaipur organized. Not all parties were formal, there was also much fun and laughter when informal parties were organized. Pictures show a few of those parties.

through the ages were always associated with power struggles and intrigues and at times there was a parallel *darbar* here that wielded as much power as the maharaja's *darbar*. Favorite *maharanis* and their maids were known to cause several upheavals in the way they made courtiers dance to their tune, sometimes bestowing favors on some and sometimes punishing others.

When Maharani Gayatri Devi came to Jaipur the *zenana* was bustling and full of life. As per tradition, each of the three *maharanis* had her own apartments with several maids and *nadars* (eunuchs) living there. Each apartment was a complete unit in itself with a *darbar* hall where the ladies

gathered on special occasions. There was laughter, music and activity there as the women held *mehfils* (get-togethers) to mark the special festivals and gathered on other occasions like birthdays and functions related to childbirth. These women hardly ever needed to go out or interact with outsiders. The *zenana* of Maharaja Sawai Madho Singh, father of Maharaja Man Singh II was known for the number of attendants that lived there. Rajmata remembers that in the year of her marriage there were some 400 women still living there, "There were widowed relatives and their daughters as well as servants and attendants; the Dowager Maharani and her retinue of ladies-in-waiting, maids, cooks, and other servants. All the retainers of the late Maharaja's other wives could not be dismissed just because their mistress had died, and so they remained the responsibility of the Ruling family."

One section of the *zenana* was given exclusively to the third Maharani and it became her own domain where she was free to entertain and hold *pujas* and meet with Rajput ladies of the *thikanas*. On her birthday every year, whenever she was in Jaipur she held a *durbar* in the *zenana* where a *puja* was held and women came dressed in their traditional Rajasthani *paushaks* and participated in the religious function held for her health and longevity.

154 and 155 The fancy dress parties organized by Maharani Gayatri Devi were a great draw and people looked forward to being invited. Ayesha managed to lighten the atmosphere by participating in all the activities herself and encouraging her guests to do the same. Pictures show a few of those memorable fancy dress parties in Cooch Behar as well as Jaipur.

The fancy dress parties organized by Maharani Gayatri Devi

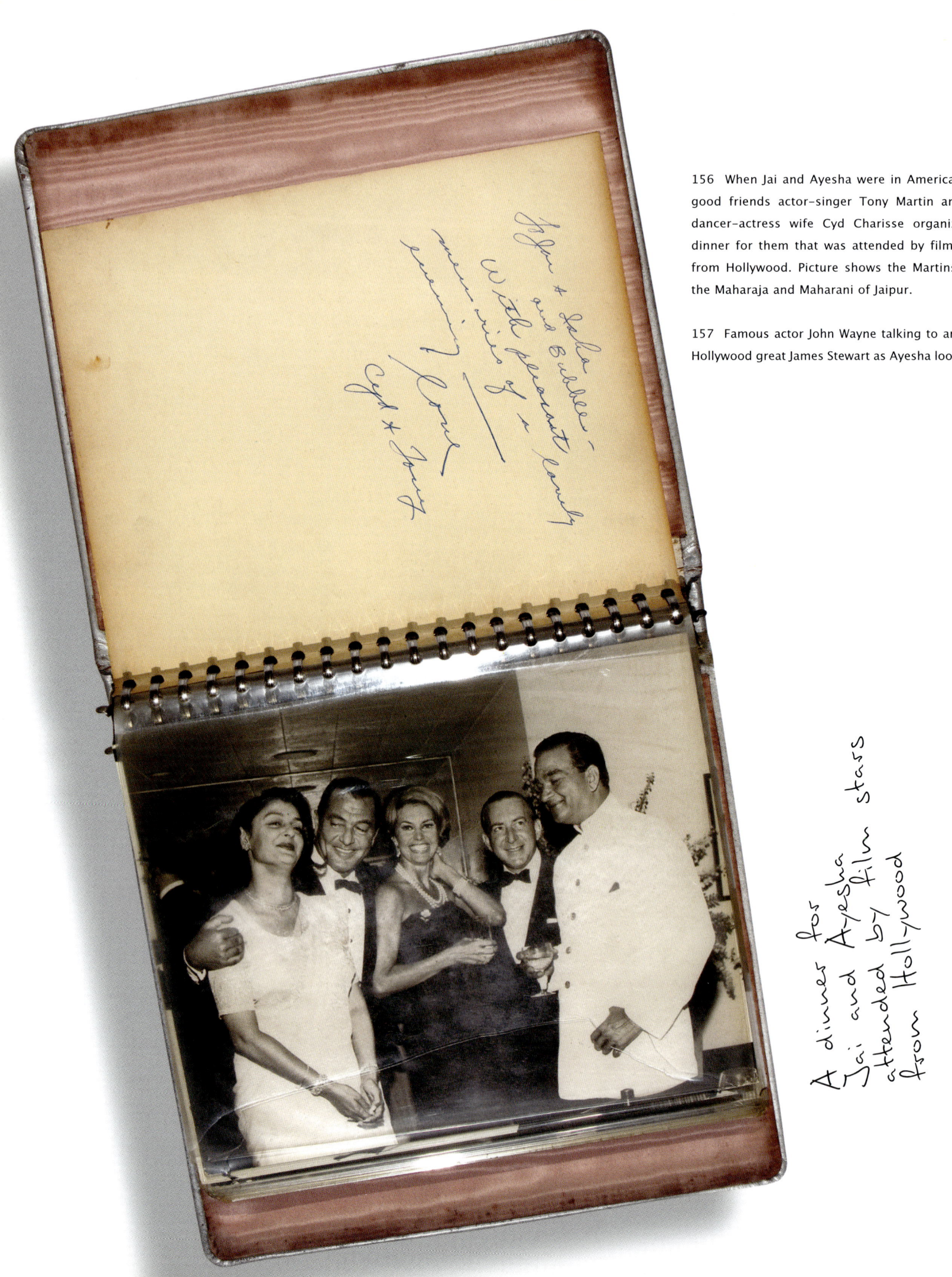

156 When Jai and Ayesha were in America their good friends actor-singer Tony Martin and his dancer-actress wife Cyd Charisse organized a dinner for them that was attended by film stars from Hollywood. Picture shows the Martins with the Maharaja and Maharani of Jaipur.

157 Famous actor John Wayne talking to another Hollywood great James Stewart as Ayesha looks on.

A dinner for Jai and Ayesha attended by film stars from Hollywood

158 The beautiful Ayesha was the centre of attraction and seemed to draw celebrity guests to her table, here host Tony Martin looks on as actor Danny Kaye talks to Ayesha.

159 The guests at every party were always keen to meet and get a chance to talk to the beautiful "Princess from India". Picture shows a guest happily posing for a picture with Maharani Gayatri Devi. Right: Ayesha on the dance floor with a guest.

160 top Jai with Cyd Charrise and Kirk Douglas.

160 bottom Maharaja Man Singh shares a joke with Edward G. Robinson. Eddy, as he was known to friends, was an honorary Academy Award-winning American actor. He is best remembered for his roles as a gangster, most notably in his film *Little Caesar*.

161 American actress of stage and screen, Rosalind Russell, who was best known for her role as a fast-talking newspaper reporter in the Howard Hawks comedy *His Girl Friday* chats with Maharani Gayatri Devi.

A New Role for the Maharani

But her life did not just centre on the *zenana* and its activities. There was much more that the Maharani was occupied with. She became involved in the All India Women's Conference, and given her interest in sports she revived the Ladies Club and encouraged its members to participate in its activities. Gradually, some of the *thikana* ladies who interacted with the Maharani regularly brought about a change in their own lifestyles just to be able to keep pace with the new and revolutionary Maharani. She did not encourage just the members of her sports clubs but also other talented youngsters. Countless ball boys, caddies and common linemen, and even gardeners who showed promise were immediately picked up for further training and given monetary assistance and a chance to train under experts, even if it meant sending them out of the country.

While Maharani Gayatri Devi was involved with her school, the Ladies Club and its varied activities, Maharaja Man Singh was spending a lot of time attending to matters of the state as the Rajpramukh. Years later he

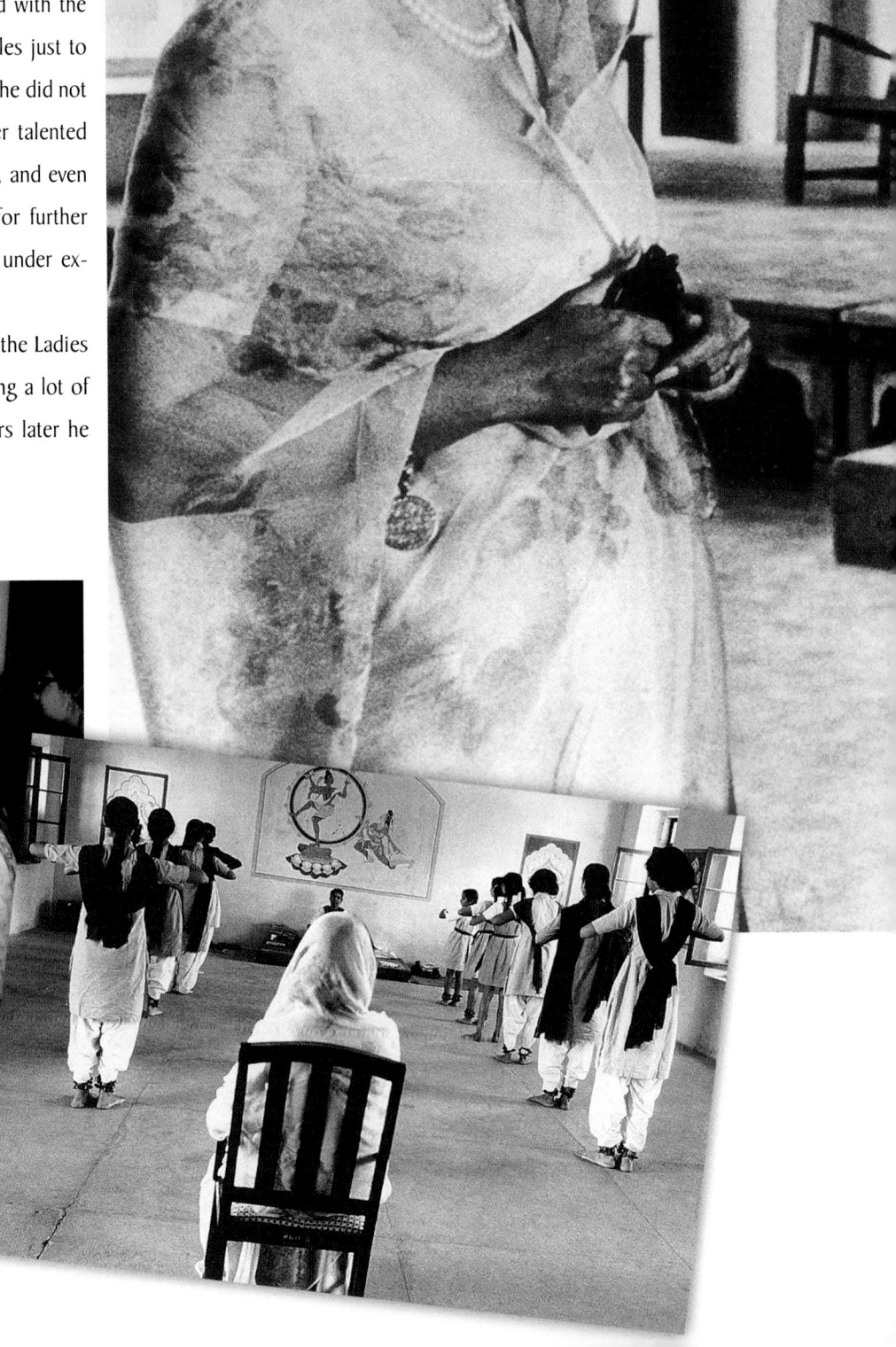

162 and 163 Coming into a traditional *purdah* (veil)–ridden state threw up a lot of challenges for the educated young Maharani and one of the first things that she did was set up a school for girls. It was named the Maharani Gayatri Devi Girls' Public School after her. She visited the school very of-ten and interacted with the students.

164 Laying the foundation stone was an essential ritual – also the first and most important ceremony before actual construction of a new building could start. Picture shows Maharani Gayatri Devi
conducting a *puja* on one such occasion.

would be recognized as the Founder of Modern Jaipur and he and his team of officers looked into every aspect of the state from roads, schools, colleges, hospitals, post offices and problems related to water and electricity. Even when India's first election took place in 1952, the new aspiring politicians of the region consulted Maharaja Man Singh. He was a much-respected man and loved by the people of Jaipur.

However, this state of affairs did not last too long as the political scenario was changing very rapidly. In October 1956, Maharaja Man Singh received letters from President Rajendra Prasad, Prime Minister Pandit Jawaharlal Nehru and the Home Minister Shri Vallabhbhai Pant informing him that he would cease to be Rajpramukh from October 31, 1956, despite the fact that he had been assured of this post for several more years. This was as unexpected as it was abrupt but didn't really surprise Maharaja Man Singh, yet he was very hurt by the shoddy way it had been handled. Being a far-sighted man he knew that this was just the beginning of the drastic changes that were to follow so he brought about some more changes in his lifestyle. He decided to turn Rambagh Palace into a hotel and moved

to Rajmahal Palace with Maharani Gayatri Devi in 1958. This action drew a lot of criticism from the other princes but it was a very bold step that was later emulated by almost every maharaja in Rajasthan.

Rajmata remembers that time very well, "When HH told us that he would be turning Rambagh into a hotel, we were absolutely stunned. Rambagh had always been home to me from the time I arrived in Jaipur, the centre of my activities and of my allegiance. But HH said that we had another home that we could move to but Jaipur needed a good hotel. I also felt very bad for Jo *Didi* because I knew she would be equally devastated at leaving Rambagh."

However, as things turned out Jo *Didi* did not have to move out of Rambagh, she passed away after a brief illness just before they were scheduled to leave for Rajmahal, their new home. There was a period of mourning that followed the Second Her Highness's death and this made their last few days in Rambagh rather painful.

Things were changing quite rapidly all around them. Even the Jaipur that Maharani Gayatri Devi had come to 20 years ago as a young bride

165 A lot of public buildings including hospitals and colleges owe their existence to Maharaja Man Singh who was known as the father of modern Jaipur. One of Gayatri Devi's duties as the Maharani of Jaipur was to lay the foundation stone of all new buildings planned by the Maharaja.

did not seem the same. Preserving the heritage of the city did not seem to be a priority with the Congress government in Rajasthan. There seemed to be total indifference. Gone were the days when the Maharaja would personally look into all aspects of the beautification and smooth running of the city. This and the fact that the Congress at the centre had behaved very shabbily with her husband put her off politics, mainly the Congress party. She hated what was happening to her beloved city and wished somebody would stop this mindless destruction. For her the final straw came when some insensitive government official ordered the demolition of the city gates. She tried to stop the work and when she didn't get a proper response from the local authorities, she immediately shot off a letter to Prime Minister Jawaharlal Nehru and requested him to intervene. Fortunately for Jaipur, Nehru instructed Mohanlal Sukhadia, the Congress Chief Minister to stop the work immediately. The royal family's love for Jaipur and the citizens had not diminished in any way at all; it was just that they now had no official role or authority in the present set-up.

They decided to concentrate on something that they had complete control over. After moving out of Rambagh the other major task that they undertook was to set up the City Palace Museum and open it to the public. There had never been any need to empty out the countless store rooms and catalogue the priceless antiques. For them these were just their personal treasures that had accumulated over the centuries and were in the family's custody: Persian carpets, historically important weapons from the Mughal period and beyond, an amazing collection of miniature paintings, priceless jewelry, furniture, crystal and cut glass, sculptures, textiles, manuscripts and countless other valuable items. The palace staff was instructed to pull out everything from the store rooms and seeing the huge quantity some items were disposed of while some were cleaned and restored for display.

A lot of effort and planning went into setting up this rare museum and it was thanks to the efforts put in by the family that the City Palace was soon recognized as one of the finest private museums in the country. A reputation it continues to hold to this day.

166–167 When Maharani Gayatri Devi joined politics and stood for election from Jaipur it gave her a chance to travel extensively within Rajasthan. She loved meeting people and talking to them about her party – the Swatantra Party.

168 and 168–169 The beautiful City Palace was the venue for many a party and saw a lot of formal dinners and dances. Each event was meticulously planned and foreign guests were always fascinated by the sheer grandeur of the palace interiors and the pomp and show that accompanied such functions.

170 Maharaja Man Singh meets the Shah of Iran during the latter's official visit to India (top). Maharaja Man Singh, the Indian Ambassador to Spain on an official visit as he chats with President Franco in Madrid (bottom).

170-171 At an official party in New Delhi with the President of India – Dr Rajendra Prasad (extreme left) and the visiting dignitary Marshal Tito being introduced to Maharani Gayatri Devi.

The Maharaja's Fourth Son

172 and 173 Maharaj Kumar Jagat Singh, the fourth son of Maharaja Man Singh was born on October 15, 1949 and though born in Mumbai, his birth was celebrated with great fanfare in Jaipur. He is seen here as a baby and with his mother – Maharani Gayatri Devi.

In October 1949, Maharaja Man Singh became the Rajpramukh, or Head of State of Rajasthan and on the 15th of the same month she gave birth to her only son Maharaj Kumar Jagat Singh. Maharani Gayatri Devi had gone to her mother's home in Mumbai for the delivery and stayed there for a month.

When news of the Maharaja's fourth son reached Jaipur there was much jubilation and people headed towards Rambagh, their official residence. Gayatri Devi recalls, "Although Jaipur was no longer a princely state, the Chief Minister of Rajasthan declared a public holiday and cannons were fired to commemorate the birth of the baby boy. People from all walks of life came to Rambagh to congratulate the Maharaja, likening him to King Dashratha of the epic Ramayana who also had four sons."

Jagat was an affectionate child and being the youngest he was close to his parents and pretty much in awe of his father. He spent his initial years in Jaipur but when it was time to go to school, like his older brothers, he was sent to a preparatory school in England. He then divided his time between England and India.

In 1962, when Jagat had just entered his teens, Maharani Gayatri Devi fought her first election and remembers that it was Jagat who phoned her from England to tell her that she had won the election by the largest majority ever.

Jagat grew up to be a very good looking and handsome young man and married Priyanandana Rangsit, a Thai princess. The young couple traveled a lot and spent their time between Thailand and Jaipur. Unfortunately the marriage did not last and within a few years they just drifted apart and headed for a divorce. The couple had two children – Lalitya Kumari Singh born on February 3, 1979, and Devraj Singh born on January 13, 1981.

When Jagat died in 1997, Rajmata Gayatri Devi was shattered and never really recovered from this blow.

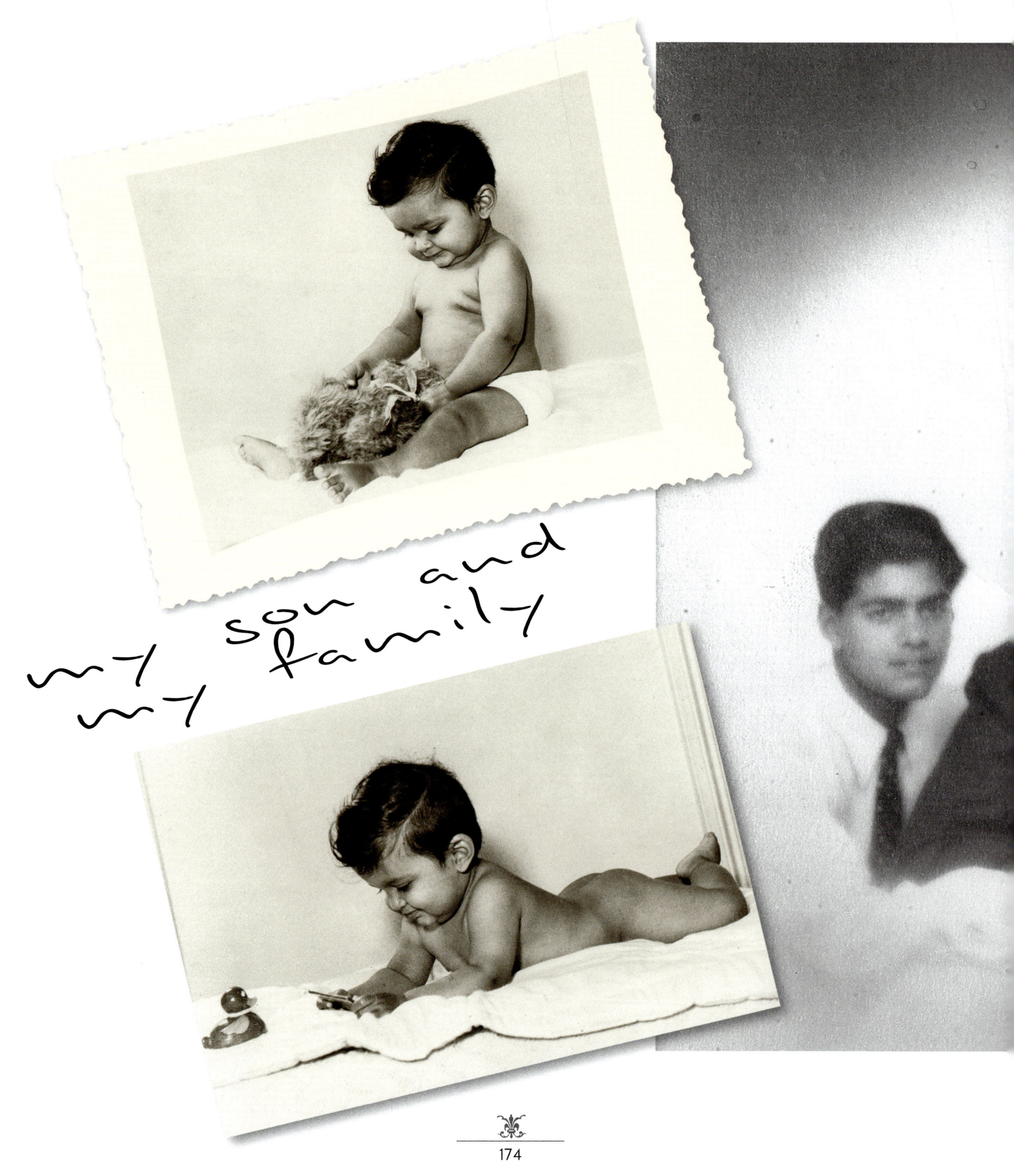

my son and
my family

174 and 174–175 Jagat as a baby and a family portrait taken in London in the early 1950s – Maharaj Kumar Jai Singh, Maharaja Man Singh, Maharaj Kumar Jagat Singh, Maharani Gayatri Devi, Maharaj Kumar Bhawani Singh and (standing) Maharaj Kumar Prithviraj Singh.

176 Jagat was a sweet baby and had his mother's looks. He was an affectionate child and very close to his parents. Here he poses for a photograph in a London studio.

176-177 Maharaj Kumar Jai Singh (Joey) and Maharaj Kumar Bhawani Singh with Jagat and Maharani Gayatri Devi and Second Her Highness Maharani Kishore Kanwar. This memorable picture was taken on the occasion of Joey's birthday.

177 Jagat and Maharani Gayatri Devi pose for a photograph in Jaipur.

178 Jagat grew up watching his family participate in all kinds of sports from polo to tennis. Here Jagat tries his hand at croquet with the governess looking on; (bottom left) trying to hit a tennis ball with a racquet almost as big as him! (center) being led away by his mother and (right) the fond mother looks on as Jagat plays with his father's riding whip.

179 The young sportsman-in-the-making Jagat ready to take a shot at the croquet balls.

180 and 181 Jagat frequently traveled with his parents and was always fascinated when they had to go by air. In these pictures he plays with a miniature toy plane that has been given to him by the airline staff as the indulgent parents look on.

182–183 Jagat celebrated his birthday in Rambagh with his mother Maharani Gayatri Devi looks on. This photograph is probably dated mid-1950s.

A TASTE OF POLITICS

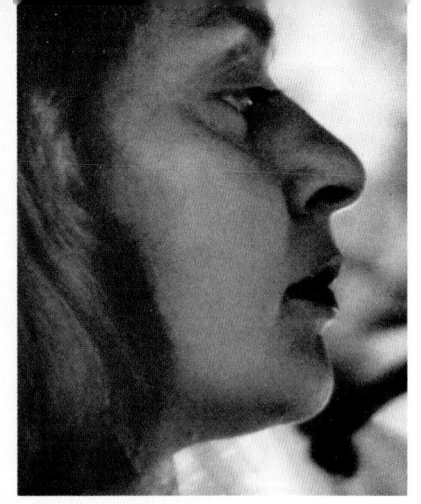

1960-1965

"She has an excellent brain and a capacity for hard work. She has for ten years represented Jaipur in parliament. Jaipur with its pink palaces full of incredible treasures, tiger infested green hills, marble rocks and atmosphere of mystery, is a fitting background for someone so exquisite…"
Barbara Cartland

The changes that had already begun sweeping through the state towards the end of the Fifties made Maharani Gayatri Devi realize that though she had never taken politics seriously nor considered it as an option it might not be such a bad idea after all. At least it would give her an opportunity to do something for the people. But which party? This was a question that bothered her because she did not wish to be associated with the Congress party.

The answer came soon enough on a trip to Mumbai to meet her mother. She heard friends discussing a new party that had been started by one of the most respected politicians of that time – C. Rajagopalachari or Rajaji as he was better known. As a close associate of Mahatma Gandhi, this elder statesman had been the unanimous choice as the Governor General of India to take over from Lord Mountbatten. He was one of the several leaders who had been disillusioned with the Congress party and had broken away to start his own Swatantra Party. As Rajmata said, "Rajaji agreed with Gandhi's view that the best government is the one that interferes least with the lives of its citizens. For all of us, the Swantrata Party and Rajaji's intelligent realism seemed like an island of sanity in the turbulent political seas around us."

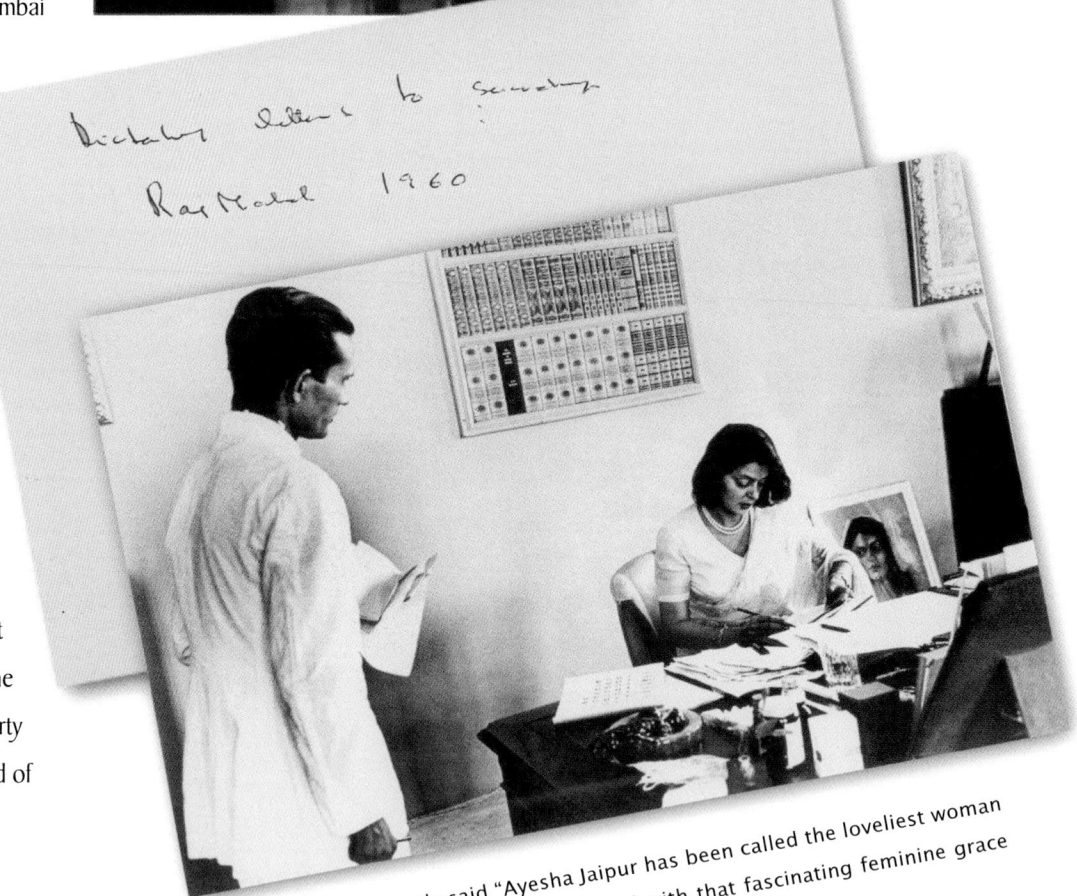

184 The charismatic Maharani Gayatri Devi looks on during one of her election rallies. The press covering her campaign was unanimous in proclaiming her a winner when they saw the crowds that gathered to hear and see her.

187 Noted writer Barbara Cartland had rightly said "Ayesha Jaipur has been called the loveliest woman in the world. She is, when one sees her, breathtakingly beautiful with that fascinating feminine grace that is characteristic of Indian women."

188 and 189 Maharani Gayatri Devi took her role as a politician very seriously. She worked out of her office in Raj Mahal Palace and personally responded to all letters and cleared pending files.

Maharani Gayatri Devi had met Rajaji during his visit to Jaipur in his official capacity as the Governor General in 1949 and remembered him as a simple but very learned and impressive personality. She could also relate to him because on this visit he had asked Maharaja Man Singh to be "vigilant because the new Government of India might not appreciate the need to preserve for posterity the many historically important buildings" that the Maharaja of Jaipur had handed to the Government. Not only had the Government not kept its word about letting Maharaja Man Singh continue as the Rajpramukh but also seemed determined to isolate him as much as possible. He was not invited to official functions nor was he given any responsibility in the new set-up. The general feeling amongst the government was one of insecurity as Maharaja Man Singh was still very popular with the citizens of Jaipur and a crowd-puller wherever he went. Sometimes, much to the discomfiture of the newly elected leaders, they were completely ignored and brushed aside while the Maharaja was almost mobbed.

With her mind almost made up to join the Swatantra Party, Maharani Gayatri Devi waited for the right time.

Meanwhile, in the summer of 1960, they learnt of Queen Elizabeth's proposed visit to India in the beginning of 1961 and being personal friends of the British royal couple, Maharaja Man Singh immediately wrote off a letter inviting her to include Jaipur in her itinerary. When the Queen gave her consent the next few months saw a lot of hectic activity as proper arrangements had to be made for the visit. Though it was to be an informal visit there were still several months of meticulous planning and back-up plans in case any last minute changes were required. Officers were given special du-

ties and told to get enough practice so that the visit went off smoothly.

The Queen's visit and the fact that she would be spending two days with the Jaipur royal family did not please the governments both at the centre and in the state. Finding themselves helpless in interfering with what was clearly a private trip, they tried to impose restrictions wherever they could, sometimes asking the Maharaja not to hold a formal *durbar* when they learnt he had plans to; sometimes asking him to ensure that no live bait was used for the tiger shoot in Sawai Madhopur. The guidelines continued for months and the preparations too continued in Jaipur.

In the midst of all this excitement, and in a classic case of bad timing, just a few days before the arrival of the Queen, Maharani Gayatri Devi officially joined the Swatantra Party. She remembers the day well as Pat was getting engaged that morning to her niece Devika Devi, daughter of her sister, Ila Devi. She just got up that morning and asked a still half-asleep Maharaja Man Singh if she could join the Swatantra Party. After he gave his approval she promptly went out to look for the ADC on duty and instructed him to invite the local secretary of the Swatantra Party for breakfast. It was as simple as that!

When the secretary arrived she made enquires and on hearing that all she had to do was pay a nominal sum towards membership fees and fill in a form she did both. Pat was there to meet her before leaving for City Palace for his engagement and decided to join the party as well and he too filled in the form. That done they both left for the City Palace. She had been toying with the idea for almost a year but the timing was spontaneous and she had no clue what it would entail.

190 and 191 The single star was the symbol of the Swatantra Party and to this day Rajmata remembers the slogans that her party workers shouted during her election meetings. Campaigning was both exhausting and interesting as the Maharani traveled to remote villages. Right she addresses a village gathering. The rural folk were totally fascinated by the beautiful Maharani and always thronged to her meetings to see her more than hear what she was saying!

Royal Duties

The Queen arrived with her entourage on January 23, 1961 to a re-sounding welcome. The streets were lined with colorfully dressed people and there was much cheering and jubilation when the royal cavalcade drove to the City Palace gates. Two caparisoned elephants stood to take them in-to the palace. One journalist's account of this visit stated:

Swaying in an open golden howdah, atop the 13 ft. elephant, The Queen, in white faille, sat beside the Maharajah. The Duke followed on a second elephant. The elephants were swathed in cloth of gold and silver chain mail with silver bells on their trunks. Seven storeys up in the gallery of a floodlit tower a band played as The Queen stepped down on to the dismounting platform, and the elephants lifted their trunks in salute." The journalist had never seen anything like this before and went on to say: *"It was an occasion of almost unbelievable splendour when the India that greeted The Queen's grandfather fifty years ago came alive again."*

When the procession reached the courtyard of City Palace there were over 100 nobles, all fully clad in their ceremonial dress, complete with long coats (*achkans*) with shining medals, starched, colorful turbans, cer-emonial swords by their side, all lined up to greet the royal couple. Everything went off smoothly, exactly as planned and there was a collective sigh of relief that there had been no mismanagement at any point. Rajmata

192 and 193 When Queen Elizabeth and Prince Philip arrived in India in early 1961 on their first official trip after Independence it did not surprise anyone when they included Jaipur in their itinerary. It was a private vis-it to meet their friends Jai and Ayesha. Pictures show Prince Philip being welcomed in Jaipur.

noted in her memoirs: *"The Queen's visit turned out to be a great success. The reception at the City Palace was really brilliant. As the Queen drove down streets accompanied by Jai, while Prince Philip followed in the next car with Bubbles, the people of Jaipur came out in all their colourful finery to greet them…The pink courtyard of the City Palace was lined with elephants, camels, horses and gorgeously decorated bullock-carts, and it was there in the audience pavilion that I received Her Majesty. I had seen many grand occasions at the City Palace, but this, I thought was the most spectacular, with the brocaded costumes of the nobles and the gold and silver trappings of the elephants blazing under all the extra television lights."*

194–195 and 195 The Queen was given a spectacular reception by Maharaja Man Singh and the people of Jaipur; no effort was spared to welcome the Royal Guest. Pictures show the Queen and Maharaja Man Singh on elephant back, on their way to City Palace; and the Royal Couple with their hosts.

196 and 196–197 The beautiful City Palace was a befitting venue for a grand reception or *darbar* that was attended by all the important people of Jaipur – from nobles to local politicians. The Royal Couple were given a traditional welcome and met with the dignitaries from the city.

The Queen. Duke of Edinburgh. H.H. & Self.

After this grand reception the royal couple went to Rajmahal Palace for dinner. The same excellent organization and management continued when the Queen and the Duke headed for Sawai Madhopur after dinner. This trip was a little more informal as there were just the immediate family members, Maharaja Man Singh, Maharani Gayatri Devi and their four sons. The only non-family member who accompanied them on this trip was Colonel Kesri Singh, the *shikar* specialist who was closely associated with Maharaja Man Singh as his ADC and in charge of the *shikarkhana* or hunting department. Popularly known as 'Tiger Man' due to his great love and understanding of the tiger, he wrote books on the tiger and hunting and even had a springing tiger painted on his white car. He was not only a very proficient *shikari* but also a great story-teller with a store house of hunting tales that he related in his inimitable style. There couldn't have been a better person to accompany the guests on this hunting expedition. Even if the *shikar* expedition was unsuccessful, Colonel Kesri Singh could be counted upon to keep the guests thoroughly entertained.

198–199 and 199 The Royal Couple did not spend the night in Jaipur, instead Jai, Ayesha and their four sons took the Queen and Prince Philip to their hunting lodge in Sawai Madhopur. The Prince did manage to bag a tiger while the Queen happily looked on. Pictures show the Queen's visit to Sawai Madhopur.

As it turned out Prince Philip did manage to bag a tiger after two unsuccessful attempts. There was much jubilation in the camp. Rajmata remembers this hunting trip for its relaxed informality: *"On the first day, the Duke of Edinburgh bagged a large tiger with a beautiful shot, after which we had a picnic lunch and then drove through the jungle looking at wild game. The dinners at the shooting-lodge were easy and amusing with Colonel Kesri Singh entertaining everyone with outlandish stories of shoots he had been on. He had insisted on wearing a red velvet smoking jacket made from a curtain said to have belonged to Queen Victoria, which he had bought at an auction in Bognor Regis. He was quite unable to resist the temptation of telling her Majesty that he was wearing her great-great grandmother's curtains!"*

200 and 201 There was more to their friendship than a common love for polo. Prince Philip was a good polo player himself and there were several occasions when he found himself playing against his friend Jai and inadvertently the winner's trophy was handed over by Jai's wife Ayesha! When Prince Philip was not playing himself he was on the fields watching his friend Jai play polo. The Queen too was often there for the important matches.

The Die Is Cast

From Sawai Madhopur the royal visitors continued on with their Indian tour and it was time for Maharaja Man Singh and Maharani Gayatri Devi to return to Jaipur. The Queen's visit had kept Gayatri Devi very involved so she hadn't had much time to follow up on her Swatantra Party membership and take the matter further. One of the first things she did upon her return to Jaipur was to write a letter to Rajaji to inform him that she'd joined his party. Rajaji responded immediately and thanked her, he also said that she was a brave lady! Brave because joining an opposition party was so politically incorrect that it could have only complicated their al-

ready delicate relationship with the Congress party. It was an apparently anti-establishment act that could lead to political retaliation like cutting down the privileges that the princes enjoyed, the major one being the privy purse. This was an agreed upon sum of money to be given to all the princes in lieu of their merging their state into India and handing over a major part of their properties to their respective State governments. If the Congress so wanted and it very often threatened to do, it could revoke the privy purse. It was the proverbial stick with which the Congress party threatened the princes at any given opportunity.

202 Just before the Queen's visit to India in 1961 Maharani Gayatri Devi had joined the Swatantra Party and was attending party meetings whenever she was called upon to do so. Picture right shows her with the founder of the Swatantra Party Chakravarty Rajgopalacharya, or Rajaji as he was commonly known.

203 Making speeches was mandatory for a politician but it was not something that the new politician–Maharani enjoyed very much, yet she remembers not doing too badly.

For Maharani Gayatri Devi, the die had been cast and she was prepared to face the outcome of her action. Two months after the Queen's visit it was time to prepare for another important visitor – Rajaji had been invited to Jaipur by the President of the Swatantra Party in Rajasthan and this time preparations of another kind would be needed. Rather than organize his trip, Maharani Gayatri Devi, as one of the most important, in fact *the* star party member from Rajasthan, was expected to address the public in her new role. To say that Maharani Gayatri was nervous about her first public appearance would be an understatement. She spent hours agonizing about the event and was, in her words, "overwhelmed with nervousness and had a dry mouth and parched lips for days before." When she shared her anxiety with her staff, they refused to take her seriously because to them she was a bold and confident Maharani who could any tackle situation with her customary poise. What if, she wondered aloud, nobody turned up at the public meeting? That fear was immediately put to rest by her lady-in-waiting who assured her that Jaipur is such a small town where people would gather even if two monkeys danced! Not a very complimentary or reassuring example but it certainly lightened the atmosphere.

This meeting in April 1961 marked Maharani Gayatri Devi's first foray into active politics. She took the microphone, appearing quite confident and in control, and welcomed Rajaji to Jaipur and invited him to address the gathering. Rajaji's speech was openly critical of the Government and well received by the public. Maharani Gayatri Devi was encouraged to know that there were more people who felt so strongly about the Government's policies and that she hadn't really done anything wrong by joining hands with the opposition party.

A month later, as had been customary for the family, they headed for London to spend their summer months there. Life continued as usual with Maharaja Man Singh playing a lot of polo and spending time with young Jagat who was in school there, while Maharani Gayatri Devi was the perfect hostess who entertained their friends in England and accompanied him to parties that usually followed during the polo season; being in England also meant being away from the heat of Rajasthan and also from the changing political scenario. It was almost like old times where they could spend time with friends and not worry about being politically correct.

Within a year of her maiden political speech in 1961, the Indian general elections were announced. In 1962, India would hold her third general elections after the earlier two of 1951 and 1957. There was hectic political activity and it was unanimously decided by the Swatantra Party that not only would Maharani Gayatri Devi be the candidate for the Jaipur parliamentary seat but she was also given the responsibility of campaigning for the other Swatantra Party candidates from the state, two of whom were Pat and Joey.

Supported by a very able team of campaign advisors and assistants, Maharani Gayatri Devi set out on a mission that took her all across the state. She visited areas that she had never been to before and travelled through impassable dirt tracks, sometimes in a car but almost always in open jeeps. Her day started at six in the morning and continued throughout the day until very late at night. There were meetings every half hour, and they stopped at villages and met people. For the Maharani of Jaipur it was an educative experience as she saw the living conditions of people and the hardships they had to endure for survival. In the face of what she saw her own discomfort seemed a very trivial issue: *"I slept under all kinds of conditions and in all sorts of places...Bathrooms were something that I couldn't arrange, and they turned out to be almost anything – a wooden stool and a bucket of water mostly, sometimes not even that."*

204 and 205 The Maharani with her party workers – a temporary office was set up in Rajmahal Palace where the Maharani could meet with her party workers to discuss matters relating to her election campaign.

206 and 207 left As the Rajpramukh of Rajasthan Maharaja Man Singh had to perform a lot of official duties during his tenure. Maharani Gayatri Devi often accompanied him – here they are seen in some of the official functions.

207 right The Maharaja and Maharani look on as Pt. Jawahar Lal Nehru the Prime Minister of India inaugurates an exhibition.

Looking back now, that entire period of her campaign seems to be one of the most extraordinary periods of her life, it was a 'campaign of love' as it helped her know and understand the people of Rajasthan like never before and appreciate how they survived in the face of adversities. Another fall-out of the campaign was that it gave her a chance to brush up on her public speaking as she had to make speeches all the time. Maharaja Man Singh lent his support as and when needed and spoke to the people of Jaipur and told them that if they voted for their Maharani it would mean they had voted for him.

After the hectic campaigning was over it was time for the voting and one of the toughest tasks before the Maharani's campaign managers was to educate the simple villagers about the electoral process. It took a lot of convincing to make them understand that they had to vote for the star, which was the Swatantra Party's symbol. The entire family waited nervously for the results to arrive, Maharaja Man Singh hoped she would win by a decent majority for the honor of the family! There were all kinds of speculations but nobody really had any doubts about the Maharani's victory.

And what a victory!

By the time all the results came in, the margin between the Maharani and her closest opponent from the Congress grew wider and wider until it reached an astounding lead of 175,000 votes! It is not difficult to imagine what Maharaja Man Singh must have felt at that moment; it was not just a victory for the Maharani but also for the house of Jaipur. It proved beyond doubt that despite the changed circumstances the people of Jaipur continued to love and trust the ex-rulers, as both Pat and Joey also won with convincing margins.

A combined victory procession followed and people were out on the streets, on rooftops, in a mood of celebration, waving, singing and shouting slogans for the longevity of the royal family.

The period that followed gave the Maharani a chance to go to Delhi as a Member of Parliament and meet with other politicians. She made her customary first speech and also tried to be present when the Prime Minister Jawaharlal Nehru addressed the House.

208 and 208-209 Traveling through remote villages in Rajasthan was a new experience for the Maharani who saw a life she had never seen before. She remembers those days as a learning process as well as a period that got her closer to the people.

210-211 Maharani Gayatri Devi was a star attraction wherever she went. For the people she was more than a politician seeking votes, she was *their* Maharani, a person who would stand by them, somebody they could depend upon.

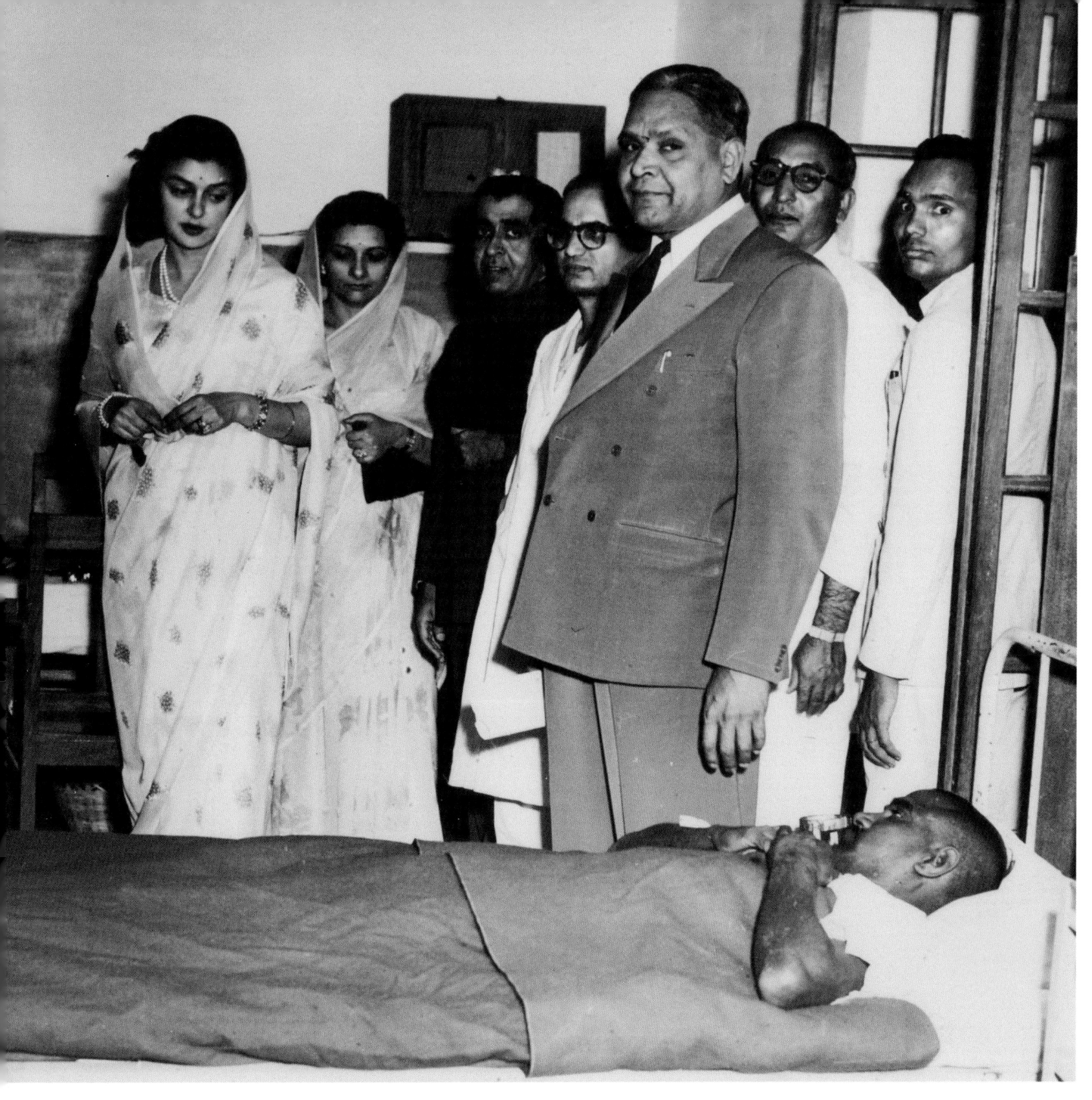

212 and 212–213 The dual duties as Maharani of Jaipur combined with those of a Member of Parliament saw an increase in the social commitments of Maharani Gayatri Devi. She is seen here attending various activities.

214 and 214–215 The Maharani chats with her young admirers on one of her election campaigns. Right a villager is keen to show his respect by garlanding her and brings her some vegetables from his farm.

216–217 For the orthodox, *purdah*-ridden women from the villages of Rajasthan it was a novelty to see their 'modern' Maharani move around freely and talk to them so openly. Little did they know that she had already started a school in Jaipur that would change the lives of women forever.

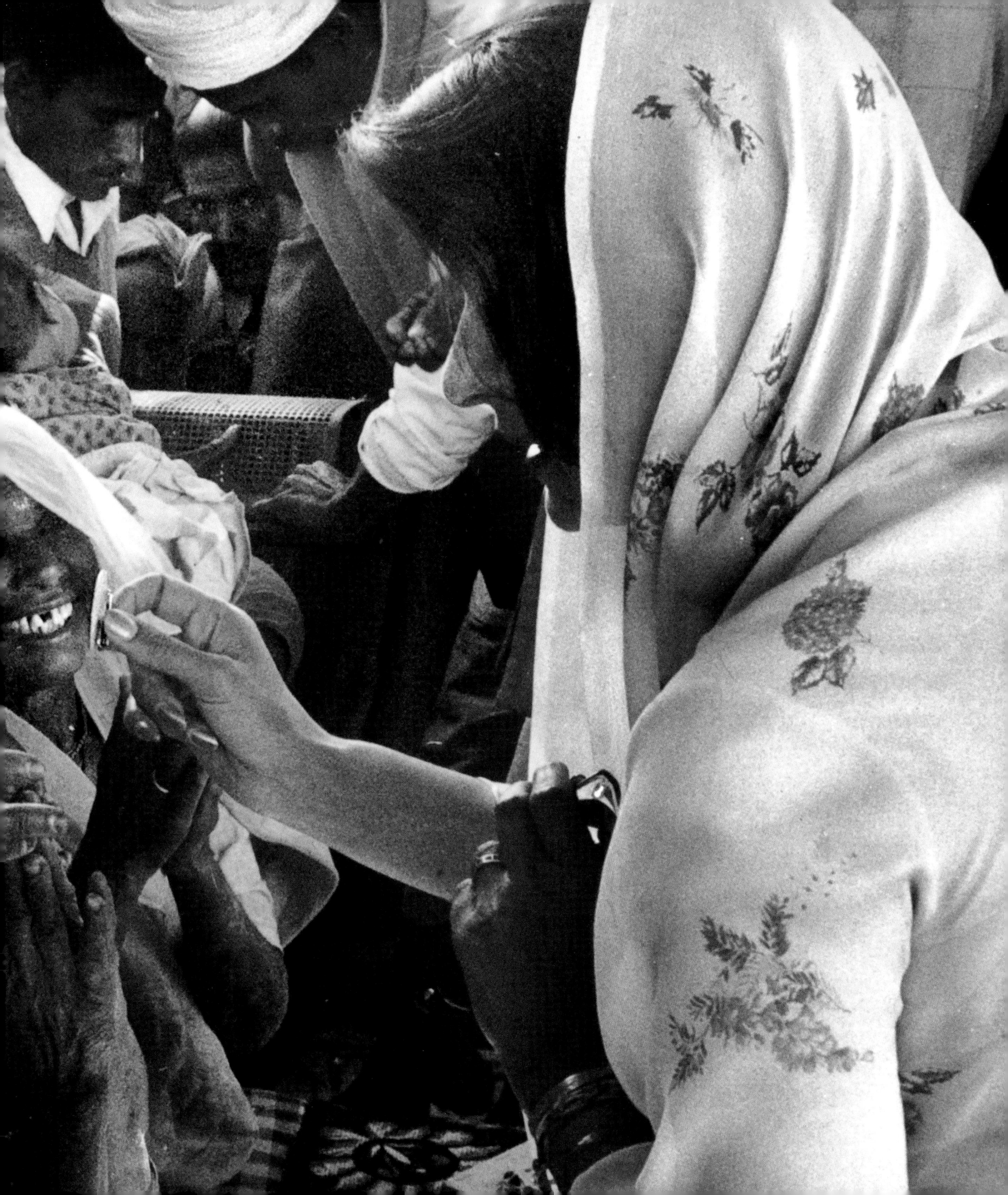

218 and 218–219 Maharani Gayatri Devi led by example – she wanted women to be educated and independent. Coming from a westernized background she thought nothing of driving her car through villages and creating a sensation wherever she went!

220-221 and 221 When Maharani Gayatri Devi traveled through villages she was a natural crowd puller but for this she gives more credit to Maharaja Man Singh. He was a very popular ruler adored by his people who would do anything for him. As his Maharani this show of respect was to be expected.

222-223 and 223 Maharani Gayatri Devi was a much sought-after chief guest and people were willing to wait for weeks until she could give them time. By the Sixties she had become such an iconic figure that admiration for her grew to huge proportions. During the election campaign Maharaja Man Singh often drove Maharani Gayatri Devi in his jeep as not all roads were accessible by car and there was a lot of cross-country driving required.

224 and 224-225 Wearing western clothes in a village, where women were not even seen in public places with their heads uncovered, was a rare sight. It was something only the Maharani of Jaipur could do! Sawai Madhopur was second home to the Jaipur family and these pictures are all from her election campaign in Sawai Madhopur.

226-227 Maharani Gayatri Devi in Sawai Madhopur during her election campaign.

228 and 229 In 1962 the Jaipur family had another very important guest – Mrs Jacqueline Kennedy, the First Lady of America and the wife of the charismatic John F. Kennedy. Though on an official tour to India, her visit to Jaipur was personal. Pictures show Maharani Gayatri Devi walking with Mrs Kennedy and on the right during a visit to City Palace with Maharaja Man Singh and Maharani Gayatri Devi.

Diplomatic Duties, Entertainment and Official Engagements

A few months later, in March 1962, it was time to receive another important guest who was scheduled to visit India in her official capacity as the First Lady of America, but her trip to Jaipur was more in her personal capacity as she had accepted an invitation from Maharaja Man Singh.

Mrs Kennedy was accompanied by her sister Lee Radziwill and the American Ambassador to India Mr Kenneth Galbraith, and despite a few 'delicate situations' where Mrs Kennedy almost did not get a chance to visit the City Palace Museum, her trip was largely successful. Later that year,

both Maharaja Man Singh and Maharani Gayatri Devi visited the Kennedys in America and came away very impressed by his "immensely attractive personality". He also introduced the Maharani as "the woman with the most staggering majority that anyone has ever earned in an election."

While they were still out of the country the first Indo China war broke out in October 1962. On their return to India there were heated debates in the Parliament and the other political parties blamed the Congress for its weak handling of the ugly situation.

230 and 230–231 Both Maharaja Man Singh and Maharani Gayatri Devi ensured that Mrs Kennedy had a wonderful time in Jaipur. Among the activities organized for her was a special polo match in her honor. Pictures show her at the polo match and posing with the winner's trophy.

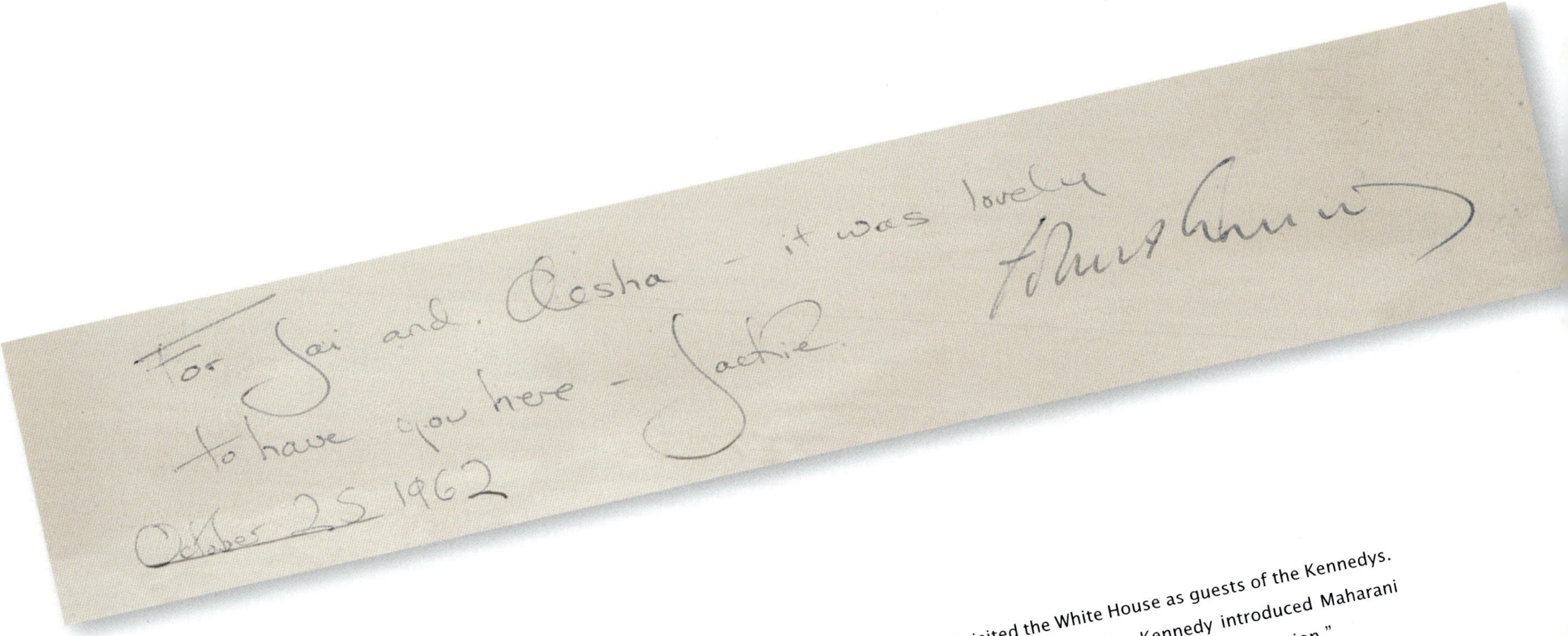

For Jai and Aesha — it was lovely to have you here — Jackie

October 25 1962

John Kennedy

232 and 233 In October 1962 both Maharaja Man Singh and Maharani Gayatri Devi visited the White House as guests of the Kennedys. They stayed at Blair House, the presidential guesthouse. It was during this visit that President John Kennedy introduced Maharani Gayatri Devi to his senators as "the woman with the most staggering majority that anyone has ever earned in an election."

234 and 234–235 Wherever they went the Jaipur royal couple was the toast of town and written about by the local newspapers and magazines who followed them with great interest.

When Pandit Jawaharlal Nehru died on May 27, 1964 after a brief illness, it was time for another change. Lal Bahadur Shastri was chosen as the next Prime Minister of India and this brought about changes for the Jaipurs as well. Shastri offered an Ambassadorship to Maharaja Man Singh and gave him a choice of three countries. Maharaja Man Singh chose Spain, and in October 1964 he left for Madrid to take up his official post.

Diplomatic duties, entertainment and official engagements which were a part of their post kept both Maharaja Man Singh and Maharani Gayatri Devi busy for the first few months; more so as he was the first Indian Ambassador to Spain. It wasn't always possible for Maharani Gayatri Devi to be present in Madrid as her duties as Member of Parliament kept her busy when the parliament was in session. But she did manage to spend as much time as possible in Madrid.

Spain was quite interesting and Maharani Gayatri Devi noted in her diary, "I must say they talk very fast in Spain! It used to drive me crazy when shopping in the department store specially while struggling to explain what I wanted. There was a loudspeaker blaring all the time. But by and large I love Spain. The people are friendly and the life is leisurely – one never seems to have to hurry – for someone like me who is always wanting to do something it is astounding how people just sit around talking!"

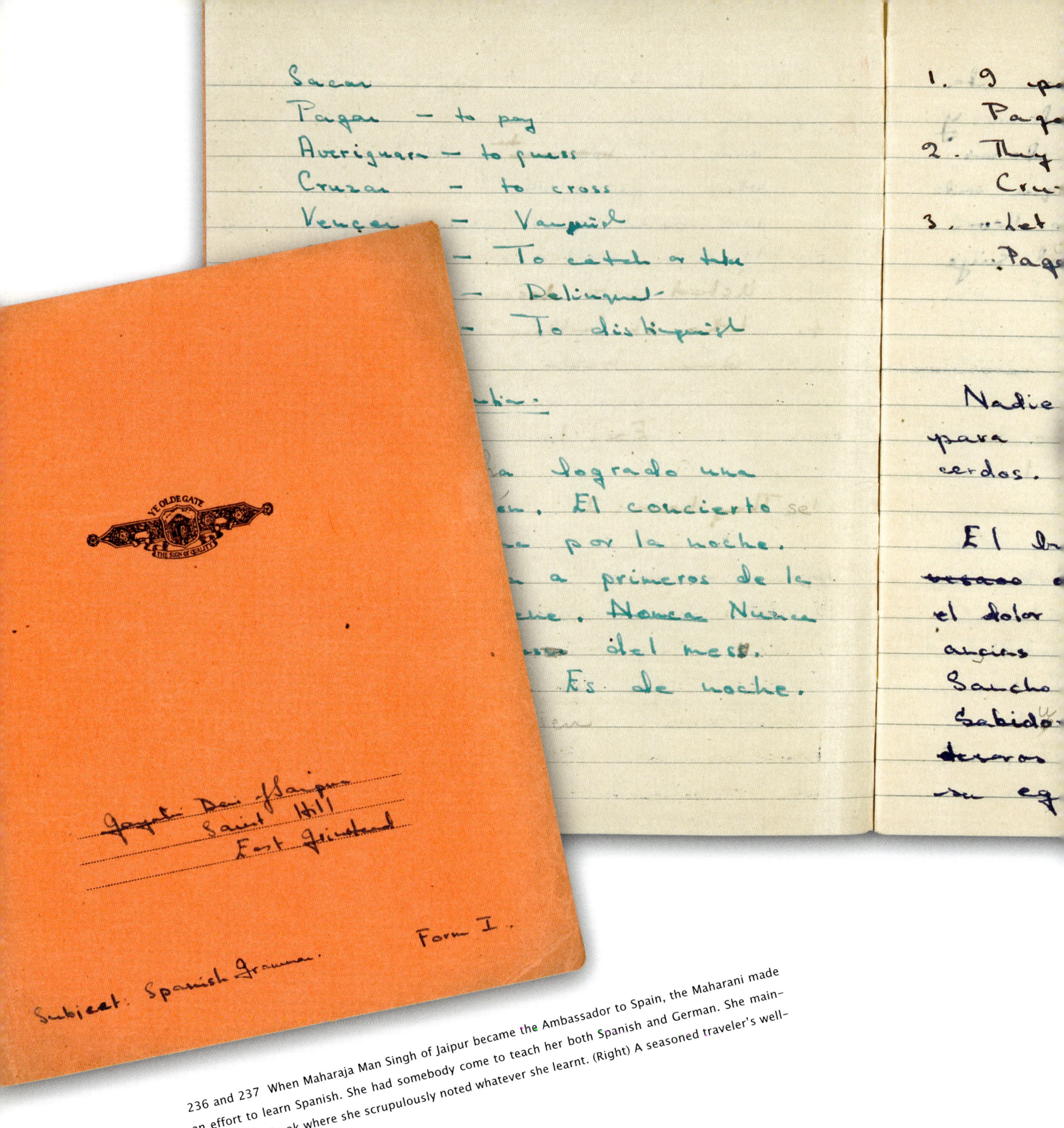

Sacar
Pagar — to pay
Averiguar — to guess
Cruzar — to cross
Vencer — Vanquish
— To catch or take
— Delinquent-
— To distinguish

logrado una
. El concierto se
por la noche.
a primeros de la
. Nunca
del mes.
Es de noche.

1. 9
Pag
2. They
Cru
3. Let
Pag

Nadie
para
cerdos.

El la
el dolor
angina
Sancho
Sabido

236 and 237 When Maharaja Man Singh of Jaipur became the Ambassador to Spain, the Maharani made an effort to learn Spanish. She had somebody come to teach her both Spanish and German. She maintained a notebook where she scrupulously noted whatever she learnt. (Right) A seasoned traveler's well-used passports.

Jayat Devi Jaipur
Saint Hill
East Grinstead

Subject: Spanish Grammar.   Form I.

238 and 239 Maharaja Man Singh, Ambassador to Spain travelled extensively throughout Europe as part of his diplomatic duties. He was almost always accompanied by his wife – the beautiful Maharani Gayatri Devi. Pictures show the royal couple during their various trips.

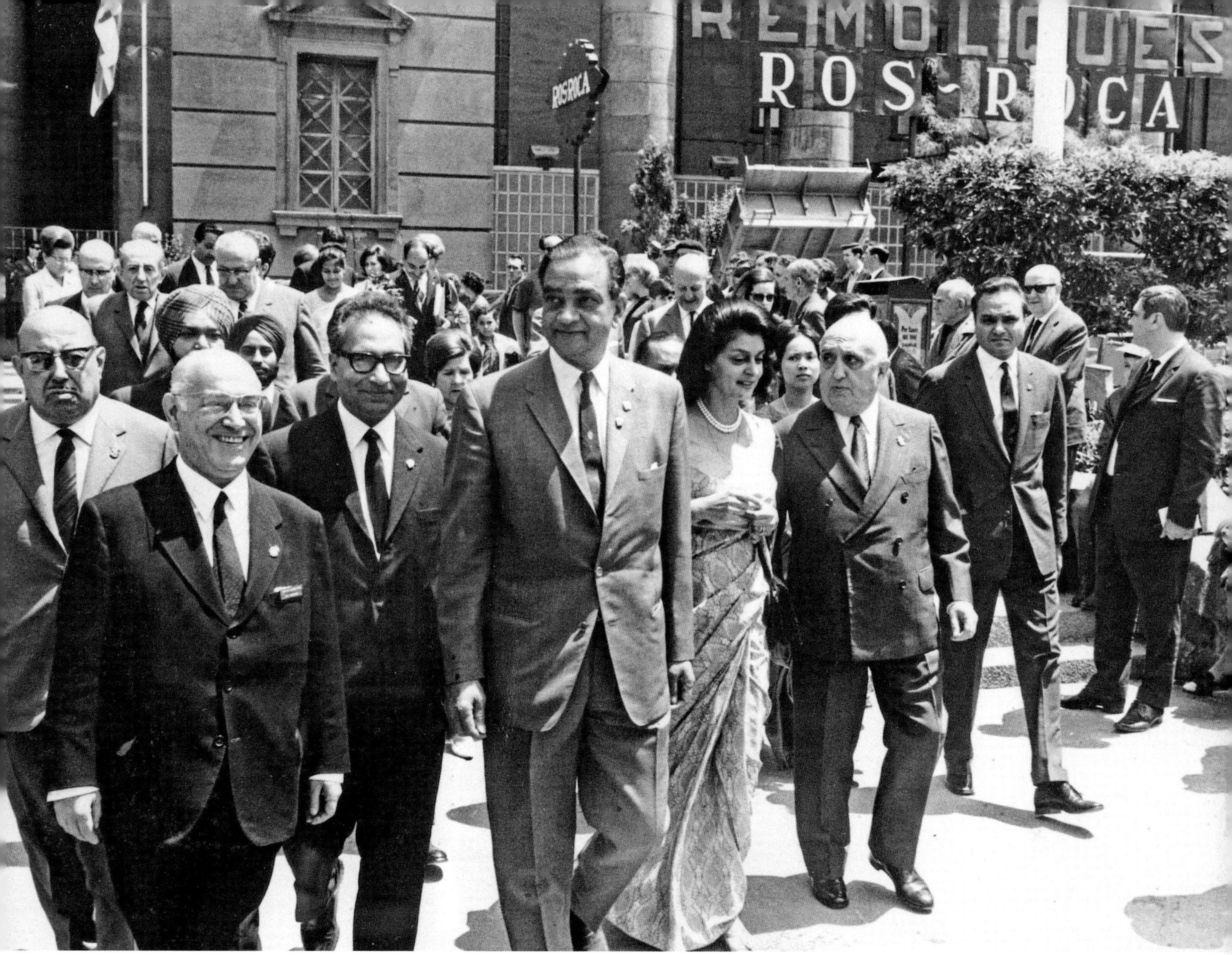
REMOLQUES
ROS-ROCA
ROSROCA

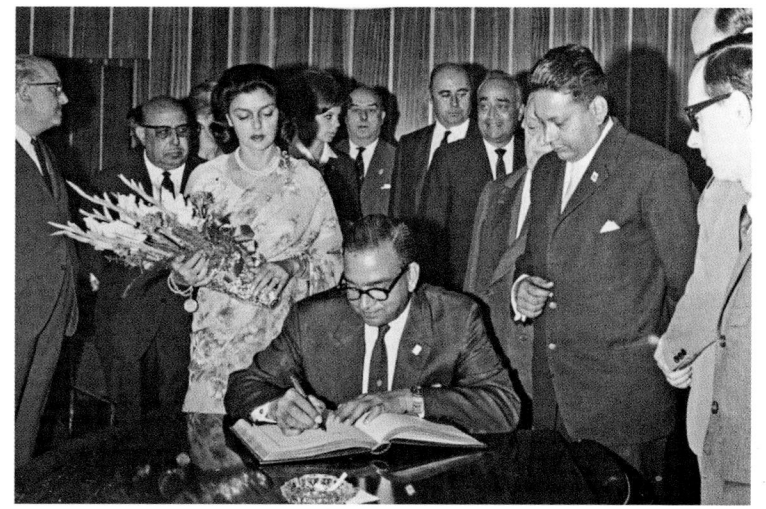

AN UNFORGETTABLE STORY

1965-2009

The year 1965 marked 25 years of marriage
and for Maharani Gayatri Devi it was "that year,
highlighted by our silver wedding anniversary,
as the last year of untrammelled happiness
and success that I have known."

240 The amazing grace and charm of the Rajmata comes across very obviously in this formal portrait taken by a Japanese photographer in Lilypool.

243 Jai and Ayesha on the dance floor during a party thrown for their silver wedding anniversary on May 9, 1965. In the same year Jai became the first Indian Ambassador to Spain and was a very popular figure there.

The entire year was one of celebrations and whenever they were together they had friends over to join them in their Silver Wedding Anniversary party while the main celebration was held in Cannes where Maharaja Man Singh happened to be visiting. Parties were also held in Spain as well as England. The anniversary party in London was perhaps one of the most extensively covered parties of that time. It was written about in almost all the major newspapers and magazines of the world. It was at this time that the US edition of Vogue magazine named Maharani Gayatri Devi as one of the 10 most beautiful women in the world; a fact that stuck to her name for the years to come when every interview, every story on her stressedthis.

244 and 245 All of 1965 was one of celebration, and friends from all over joined them in their Silver Wedding Anniversary party. Here below is shown an invitation card for the dancing party which was held at Kings Beeches.

Jai and Ayesha
request the pleasure of the company of

— — — — — — — — — — —

to celebrate their Silver Wedding Anniversary
on Saturday, the 19th June, 1965,
at Kings Beeches.

10.30 p.m. Dancing
Black Tie.

R.S.V.P.
The Secretary,
Kings Beeches,
Sunninghill,
Ascot, Berkshire.   PLEASE BRING THIS CARD WITH YOU.

246 and 247 The London Silver Wedding Anniversary party was well–attended and became one of the most–talked about parties of that year. It was covered by all the major newspapers of the world.

MOST BEAUTIFUL

THEY call **Arlene Dahl** the most beautiful woman in the world (how many is that in the last two years?).

Yesterday I decided to ask this particular most beautiful woman for HER list of the most beautiful women in the world.

Arlene doesn't think age has anything to do with true beauty.

"Some women grow more beautiful as they grow older," she said. "Inner peace is much more important than outward glitter."

After that profound statement we got down to names. Here they are, and at left, are pictures of the Proud Beauties:

Garbo: "She has a fascinating laugh and smile."

Dolores Del Rio: "She works at being beautiful."

The Maharanee of Jaipur: "Serenity and inner beauty."

Ursula Thiess (Mrs. Robert Taylor): "Beautiful and expressive eyes."

Gina Lollobrigida: "Well made, with a down-to-earth beauty."

Elizabeth Taylor: "Perfection of eyes, nose, and mouth. No other woman can compare with her."

Ava Gardner: "Animal magnetism that reaches out and captures her audience."

Fiona Campbell-Walter (now Baroness Thyssen): "She looks like rare champagne."

Maharanee.   Garbo.

Ursula.   Gina.

Ava.   Fiona.

Dolores.   Elizabeth.

SINCE Eva Bartok married, the Marquis of Milford Haven's most regular companions around the bright lights, sporting events, and social functions have been the sari-wearing Maharanee of Jaipur and her wealthy husband. The three have frequently been seen together, and if the Maharajah "can't make it," the Marquis escorts the Maharanee for him.

The Maharanee of Jaipur at Claridge's last night.

Tiaras hung as heavy as lead pipes on lacquered hair.

The King and Queen of Nepal later moved between a channel of shy guests. In the throng were Lord Lansdowne, Sir Charles and Lady Norton, Sir Geoffrey Betham, the Maharajah and Maharanee of Jaipur, Field-Marshal Lord Slim, Field-Marshal Lord Harding.

Sir Harry Brittain, carrying his inevitable shooting-stick, wondered why the King had made his Guildhall speech in Nepali.

"I had quite a long chat with him," he said. "And, do you know, he speaks better English than I do."

248 The Sixties was a period when the famed beauty of Maharani Gayatri Devi of Jaipur was written about by the International press. She was acknowledged as one of the 10 most beautiful women in the world.

249 Ayesha relaxes in the sitting room in Kolkatta. Her brother's portrait is in the background.

Campaign Trail for the Second Time

Towards the end of the year, however, another event marred the peace of the country when war broke out between India and Pakistan in September 1965. This was followed by the tragic death of Prime Minister Lal Bahadur Shastri in January 1966, who was briefly succeeded by Gulzarilal Nanda and then Mrs Indira Gandhi. It was also time for India's fourth general election in 1967. This time around Maharani Gayatri Devi was not as enthusiastic as she had been five years ago. Her fervor had considerably diminished and though she still felt committed to the policies of the Swatantra Party, she was not very happy when the party formed an alliance with the right-wing Jan Sangh party. She did understand that it was a political alliance that was necessary to provide a stiffer opposition to the Congress party. Both Joey and Pat refused, stayed away and did not wish to contest.

This period also marked the emergence of Mrs Indira Gandhi, a political leader who had gradually assumed centre stage at this time in the history of India; a leader who would play a very important part in the life of Maharani Gayatri Devi in the years to follow. Mrs Indira Gandhi, the daughter of India's first Prime Minister Jawaharlal Nehru would not only change the history of the country but also cause a lot of grief to Maharani Gayatri Devi.

Mrs Indira Gandhi, a petite and seemingly mild and gentle person emerged as such a strong and astute political figure that she surprised the old guard within the Congress party by her ability to out-maneuver opponents. She was un-stoppable, and hit the Indian political scene like nothing had done before. She was contesting the 1967 election for a parliamentary seat for the first time and was confident of taking on all opposition candidates on their home ground if necessary.

This was a very closely contested election and put a lot of pressure on the candidates as it became evident that victory would not be as easy this time around as it had been in 1962. The hectic campaigning took its toll on Maharani Gayatri Devi and she fell seriously ill at the crucial time just before the final campaigning, and had to stay away from her constituency for two weeks. However, when the results came in the Maharani had won her seat but the other successful candidates realized just how close the fight had been: the Congress party had secured 89 seats while the combined alliance of Swatantra and Jan Sangh won 95 seats. With a lead, no matter how slim, the Governor was expected to call the party with the majority to form the Government, but in an unexpected turn of events the Congress party was asked to form the Government. The disgruntled public took to the streets to show their solidarity with the Swatantra party. A curfew was imposed on the entire city and there

250 The Indian general election in 1967 was a very closely contested one. The hectic campaigning and the fact that Maharani Gayatri Devi was up against seasoned politician Indira Gandhi drew a lot of worldwide coverage, and the election campaign was written about with great interest. Left: Maharani Gayatri Devi with members of her political team. Right: leaders from the Swatantra Party in discussion during a political meeting in Jaipur.

were violent protests in the streets that culminated in a shooting that left nine people dead and several injured. President's rule was imposed and the reins of the Government handed over to the Congress party after a few winning candidates were lured into joining them to make up the desired numbers.

Already disillusioned with the new political set-up, for the Maharani this was a first-hand experience of the murkier side of politics and it didn't take her long to realize that the world that she had entered with a lot of idealistic dreams and the desire to do something for the people of Rajasthan was perhaps not what she had thought it would be. She noted in her diary on January 9, 1967: *"Nepotism and corruption have reached the limit and even beyond the limit if that makes sense and the victims as always are the innocent poor. And this from a party that claims to be socialistic!! It is ironical, sad and heartbreaking to see what is happening to the wonderful people who are Indians. Proud good people sacrificed for the greed and lust of a few. Justice does not exist. Truth is a thing to laugh at. Honesty is a fool. But hunger and want are real. If ever I give up politics it will be because it hurts so much to see all this. I could easily lose myself in the pleasures of travel and international society and bury my head like an ostrich and not look at what is happening but I love too much and too deeply. I love these people. I love those children. I want a bright future for them, they are India."*

The aftermath of the election had left a lot of scars on the hearts of people who were involved in it but the worst was yet to come. Maharani Gayatri Devi left for Spain to join her husband there and tried not to think of just how much the political arena had changed. She had already decided that she would curtail her involvement with politics and keep it to a minimum.

After Mrs Indira Gandhi took over as the newly elected Prime Minister on January 22, 1966 she was even more confident after her win in the 1967 elections. One of the first major decisions that she took was to abolish the privy purses that were being given to the princes. So in July 1967 the All India Congress Committee adopted a resolution that not only were the privy purses to be stopped but henceforth all privileges that were being given to the princes would also be discontinued. The princes throughout the country felt cheated, even betrayed. To them it was a promise broken and for months after that they had countless meetings amongst themselves and with Government representatives to resolve the issue, but for the princes it was a battle that had been lost even before it began. The Government was very clear that there was no place for Maharajas in a democratic set-up and if they wanted to survive in the new India they would have to do so as common citizens: no titles, no palaces and no special treatment.

251 Hectic public meetings and speeches took their toll on Maharani Gayatri Devi and she fell quite ill during the election campaign but she carried on regardless and attended as many meetings as she could.

The writing was clearly on the wall and the message had been driven home. It was time for Maharaja Man Singh the Ambassador of Spain, to head homewards. He had been a successful Ambassador for India and was without doubt, the right man for the job, but the trouble brewing in India over privy purses hastened his return home as he wanted to be with his fellow princes to push for their continuation. A Concorde of Princes was formed but failed to find a common ground to negotiate with the Government. The princes lost and with them India lost a very important link with the past.

Throughout the late Sixties there was a very strong feeling that the abolition of privy purses was more a personal vendetta than anything else. It was an action meant to settle scores with the strong royal ladies who had been successful as politicians, but these were stories that could never be substantiated.

It was a low period in Maharani Gayatri Devi's life. In September 1968 Ma Cooch Behar died. Maharani Gayatri Devi's political career and her constant traveling hadn't left her much time to spend with her family and she was also worried about her favorite brother Bhaiya, married to an English woman by the name of Gina Egan, who had suffered an accident a couple of years previously and hadn't really recovered. She herself fell ill a year after Ma Cooch Behar died and was recovering from an operation when news of Bhaiya's death reached her on April 11, 1970. Both Maharaja Man Singh and Maharani Gayatri Devi went to Cooch Behar and were there for the mourning period and throughout that time Gayatri Devi felt saddened by the fact that a very strong link with her childhood and her home was lost.

In May 1970, as was their annual schedule, Maharaja Man Singh left for England to be followed by Maharani Gayatri Devi a few days later. Just before he left, Maharaja Man Singh seemed a little unwell and was advised by doctors not to strain himself, but he dismissed their concern over his health. Though he had curtailed his polo playing to quite an extent due to a fall a couple of months earlier, he continued with his normal active life, attending parties and doing what he always did when he was in England. He was saving his energy for a major polo match in Cirencester on June 24, 1970.

Maharani Gayatri Devi and Bubbles were watching this fateful match when without warning Maharaja Man Singh fell off his horse. He'd suffered a massive heart attack and by the time he was rushed to hospital he'd died.

Life for Maharani Gayatri Devi seemed to come to a standstill. It was a tragedy that turned her whole life around. In a space of three years she had lost three of her most precious relatives. Suddenly she felt all alone, "I could never bring myself to come to terms with that loss. I was so used to going to him for advice that when he was not there anymore I was bereft."

Meanwhile, when news of the Maharaja's death reached Jaipur the entire city mourned. He was a well-loved and respected ruler and no matter what the Government felt about the maharajas and their role in India, he was their *annadata* (or provider) and they poured into the streets when the airplane carrying his body reached Jaipur. His body was taken to City Palace to enable people to pay homage to him. When the funeral procession started the next day it was an amazingly touching occasion with thousands of people lining the streets, caparisoned elephants, horses, camels, gun carriages, chariots, a police band and a 600-strong army. It was a befitting farewell to a great ruler. He was laid to rest at Gaitore, the royal crematorium where the rulers who had gone before him had memorial cenotaphs erected in their memory.

253 Maharaja Sawai Man Singh of Jaipur, then Ambassador to Spain, poses for a photograph under his portrait from younger days. This photograph was taken just a few months before he died.

254 A beautiful photograph of Maharani Gayatri Devi taken in Jaipur at the time of her second election campaign. She always photographed very well and was a photographer's dream subject.

Maharani Gayatri Devi was devastated and understandably so. A year later, on March 10, 1971 she noted in her diary:

"I need someone older than me, someone who cares for me. You had such high principles; no one else seems to have those standards. I'm lost and miserable without you. There is nothing to look forward to and no joy in living. In less than two years I've lost Ma, Dada and you. Life is so cruel. I had so much happiness and so much love and now nothing."

An era had ended.

Coming to terms with her grief wasn't easy but life has to go on. From Maharani Gayatri Devi she had now become Rajmata (Queen Mother) Gayatri Devi and Bubbles became the next Maharaja of Jaipur. There was a month of mourning when she stayed indoors, in her section at the City Palace. In July she left for England with younger son Jagat, then just 19 years old, for the memorial service in the Guards' Chapel. It was a deeply moving service with all their friends attending and paying tributes to their friend 'Jai'. Lord Mountbatten, 'Dicky' to the family, was there to read a tribute to him, despite his bad health.

But the bad time was not quite over yet and more tragedies followed. Jai's daughter, Mickey, whose wedding had been featured in the Guinness Book of World Records as the most expensive wedding, died at the age of 41, followed by Gautam, a favorite cousin and a childhood playmate. The last death was that of Maharaja Man Singh's older brother Bahadur Singh in Isarda, from where he had been adopted.

On the political front the stage was set for another battle. Mrs Indira Gandhi dissolved the Parliament in February 1971 and called for an election, one year ahead of schedule. Sad and lonely, Rajmata Gayatri Devi wished for nothing more than to be left alone with memories of the time when life had been so full of laughter and joy. She felt isolated and didn't care one way or another what political equations were being affected and who the winning candidates were. It had only been eight months since Maharaja Man Singh's death and she just did not feel strong enough to resume her public life again. She was shaken out of her grief by two ladies for whom she had great affection: *Rajdadisa*,

the grandmother of the Maharaja of Jodhpur and the Rajmata (Queen Mother) of Bikaner, wife of Maharaja Sardul Singh, both of whom urged her to put her grief aside and stand for the forthcoming election as people like her were needed.

Though Rajmata Gayatri Devi won this election as well, there were complaints that the electoral rolls had been tampered with. Almost the entire staff of Rambagh, City Palace and Rajmahal as well as thousands of pro-Swatantra Party Rajput voters found that their names were struck off the voting list. It appeared as if the Government was playing very safe this time as they did not wish to have the 1967 situation repeated at any cost. As expected, the Congress won with a clear majority and Mrs Indira Gandhi came back, now more confident and more powerful than ever before. Among the new policies and bills that were passed were two that would later impact the princes. In December 1971 a bill was passed by both houses of Parliament that finally abolished the privy purses and all privileges of the princes. Another seemingly innocuous bill – the infamous MISA or the Maintenance of Internal Security Act – was instituted which gave the Government the power to arrest people and imprison them without a trial for a period of one year. A lethal weapon in the hands of a Government that could use it as and when it wanted – and it did so a few years later.

Mrs Indira Gandhi was on a high and even a war with Pakistan in 1971-1972 did not weaken her position in any way. If anything, she emerged stronger than before and was soon recognized as the 'most admired woman in the world' in polls in and out of the country. This was her moment of glory and there was no stopping her now.

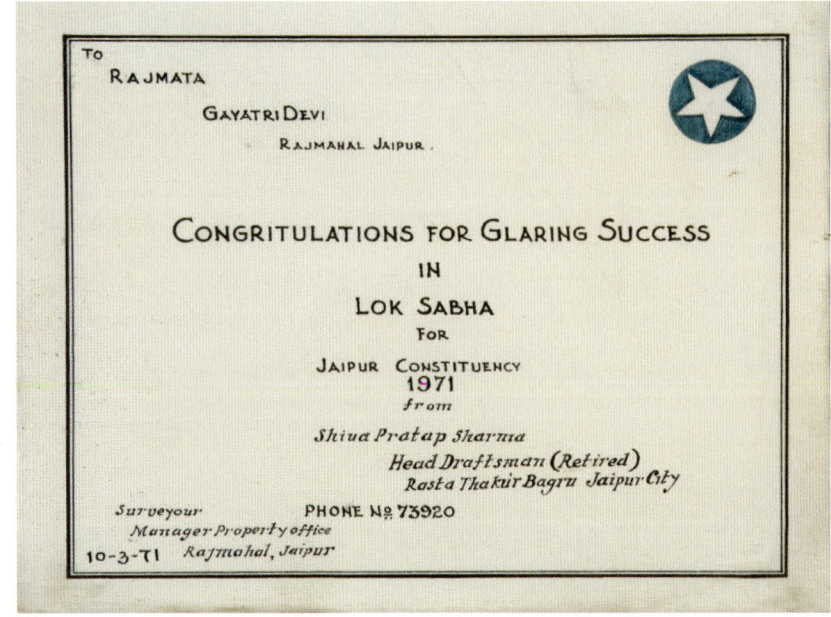

To
RAJMATA
GAYATRI DEVI
RAJMAHAL JAIPUR.

CONGRITULATIONS FOR GLARING SUCCESS
IN
LOK SABHA
FOR
JAIPUR CONSTITUENCY
1971
from

Shiva Pratap Sharma
Head Draftsman (Retired)
Rasta Thakur Bagru Jaipur City

Surveyour
Manager Property office   PHONE No 73920
10-3-71   Rajmahal, Jaipur

LOK SABHA

SUMMONS

Parliament House,
New Delhi, *January 8, 1973*
Pausa 18, 1894 (Saka)

Dear Shrimati Gayatri Devi of Jaipur,

I have the honour to inform you that the President has been pleased to
issue the following order on the 2nd January, 1973:—

ORDER

'In exercise of the powers conferred upon me by clause (1) of
article 85 of the Constitution, I hereby summon the Lok
Sabha to meet at New Delhi on Monday, the 19th February,
1973 at 11 A.M.

January 2, 1973.

V. V. GIRI,
President.'

2. I am to request you to attend the session of Lok Sabha accordingly.

Yours faithfully,
S. L. SHAKDHER,
Shrimati Gayatri Devi of Jaipur, M.P. Secretary.

256 and 257 When Rajmata Gayatri Devi won her second election in 1971 and was elected to the Lok Sabha yet again there was much jubilation and people sent her letters and cards to congratulate her (left). (Top) A summons from Mr V.V. Giri, President of India calling all members of Lok Sabha to meet on February 19, 1973. (Right) The beautiful politician–Maharani meeting people of her constituency.

Life for the princes continued as usual with stray incidents that drove home the point that they were now to be treated as common citizens like everybody else. Rajmata Gayatri Devi got a taste of this on February 11, 1975 when she was 'raided' by the income tax department who visited her residence with a search warrant that give them a right to search her home for possible hidden treasure kept there illegally. Not only her residence but every property belonging to the royal family was raided. What they did find on Rajmata's dressing table was foreign currency: 19 pounds sterling, and a few Swiss francs that were more than the permitted limit. This was reason enough to suspect the family of illegal possession of foreign currency! No case was registered but they were 'offenders' in the eyes of the law. The punishment was to come a little later.

In Delhi, there were several political upheavals but Mrs Gandhi overcame all of them until the Allahabad High Court, in a landmark judgment on June 12, 1975, annulled her 1971 election on grounds of electoral malpractice and debarred her from contesting for six years. Two weeks later, on June 25, 1975 she declared a state of Emergency and took complete charge of the Government. The Emergency saw the whole country in a state of chaos; hundreds of opposition leaders were arrested under MISA. Each morning the newspapers carried stories of how many more leaders had been jailed and how many had managed to evade arrest by going into hiding.

There was foreboding in everyone's heart that it would not be long before the Jaipur royal family found itself in some kind of trouble. And it did, a month later.

Rajmata still remembers that fateful day; "It is difficult to ever forget that afternoon on July 30th when I was woken up from my siesta at 33, Aurangzeb Road, New Delhi by one of the staff who came to tell me that two police inspectors wanted to see me. I went to the sitting room and they asked me if I was Rajmata Gayatri Devi and when I said 'yes' they promptly produced a warrant for detention under COFEPOSA or the Conservation of Foreign Exchange and Prevention of Smuggling Act. I protested saying that there must be a mistake but they said no those were their orders and I must come at once. I went into Bubbles' room and said, 'Bubbles, two policemen have come to arrest me.' He said, 'What nonsense.' I said 'No, it's true!' He came into the sitting room with me and they asked him if he

was Col. Bhawani Singh and they said they had a warrant for his arrest too. We were both speechless. Bubbles asked if we could make a phone call but they refused us that."

Rajmata Gayatri Devi and Maharaja Bhawani Singh were taken to the notorious Tihar jail. It was heartwrenching for everybody who heard about this imprisonment. Here was a Maharani who had a fairy-tale lifestyle that people only heard about but never saw for themselves, a gracious lady who had always lived a lavish life in a palace with 400 servants, who slept on the most exquisite bed linen, French silk and satin sheets, whose toiletry came from the best companies in Europe; a lady of her stature thrown into jail for the flimsiest of reasons. Was her 'crime' of possessing some foreign currency such a heinous offence that she should be thrown in jail with prostitutes and common criminals and confined to a small stinking cell with the most atrocious sleeping and toilet conditions?

People were saddened because of the unfairness of it all. Letters came from all over the world, including from their friend Lord Mountbatten, but no appeal made any difference to Mrs Gandhi.

While the rest of the world waited for good sense to prevail, Rajmata's famous grit and spirit never wavered. All her pain and tears were only for when she was alone. When she appeared outside the cell and met with other people it was as a well-composed and controlled person. The other inmates knew her as a brave and strong Maharani who was always there to help and advise. She organized books and set up a school to teach children there; she read a lot and also did a bit of embroidery to keep busy. Having got permission to walk with Bubbles in the evening, she looked forward to her evenings when she could talk to him. She endured all problems with her usual good humor and never gave a hint of her inner turmoil. The other inmates there were eager to help her and Rajmata specially remembers one of them who insisted on cleaning her room. People around her knew that grave injustice had been done but such was the fear of the dreaded Emergency that no one was willing to speak out and face the wrath of the Government and the consequences.

The Rajmata of Jaipur was joined by another royal lady, the Rajmata Vijiyaraje Scindia of Gwalior, who was also detained for some obscure reason and sent to Tihar jail. Each tried to cheer up the other and to find some humor in their bleak and dreary days.

One of the things that Rajmata did in jail was to keep a diary and note down each little incident. Both Pat and Joey and other family members took turns to visit her and it was a period of great distress for everybody. It was a nightmare and one that gave her a lot of anguish. An entry in her diary reads: "There is a deep pain in my heart – it hurts very much and there is no one to tell. In the world in which I live there is no love, no sympathy, no loving arms, no shoulder to cry on. You have to hide the hurt because if anyone saw it they would laugh and be pleased. There is no sympathy here, nor any understanding. So all my pent up feelings are hurting and there is a pain in my chest – sometimes it is such an acute pain."

Ms Urvashi Devi Baria, (ex Minister of Tourism, Gujarat), the daughter of the late Princess Prem Kumari (Mickey), visited her in Tihar and recalls one visit when she was accompanied by her two-year-old son, " We were only allowed to see her once in two weeks so we took turns to go and visit. My son was with me and on seeing the iron bars he asked, 'Have we come to a zoo?'

Grandmother (Rajmata) responded immediately, 'Yes, it is a zoo. Come in and I'll show you all the animals!' It must have been terrible for her and we just hated what she was going through but she was very brave about it and never showed any kind of discomfort and tried instead to cheer us up."

Bubbles was released after two and a half months, but the Rajmata's days in jail came to an end after five and a half months when she fell ill on January 11, 1976 and had to be hospitalized. Well meaning friends and relatives put pressure on her to write a placatory note to Indira Gandhi and speed up her release.

The days after Tihar were marked by withdrawal from the public scene for a few months. To date she does not like to talk about those stressful days. It's a closed chapter with her and one that she doesn't discuss. She only talks about the funny incidents associated with those days.

When she returned to Jaipur the family warned the public not to gather in large numbers as it could lead to problems again and as a result the celebrations were rather subdued but nothing could stop the 600-odd people who turned up to welcome her home. Though back home, there were still a lot of restrictions on her movements as she was out on parole and needed to inform the local authorities if she wanted to leave town.

259 Rajmata maintained a diary when she was in Tihar Jail. She often wrote about her jail experience and this poem talks of those days.

TIHAR
July 1975
January 1976
Stunned, bewildered, on my own
Sans family, nor friend, nor phone
Resentment seething in my heart
Not talented in any from of art
To pass the long and empty days
I spent my time in many ways
And how to help a worthy cause
Although it merits no applause
I hope this worthless 'work of art'
Will find a place at someone's heart.
Gayatri Devi of Jaipur

In 1976, India was ready for elections again but this time around Rajmata could not campaign against the Congress Party as being on parole did not allow her this right. But the 18 months of Emergency had led to a lot of resentment against Mrs Gandhi and it was that fact alone that was instrumental in routing the Congress and giving the Janta Party a landslide victory.

With the swearing in of the new Government there was almost immediate relief in the restrictions that had been imposed on Rajmata. Her passport, impounded a year earlier, was returned, the case withdrawn and she was free to travel as and when she wanted. The new Government also tried to involve her in public life all over again by nominating her the Chairperson of the newly formed Rajasthan Tourism Development Corporation in 1977, and maybe also to make amends for the way the previous Government had treated her.

It was a new role for her and one that she took quite seriously. She looked at it as an opportunity to do something for Rajasthan. Tourism in the state was a growing industry, still at its fledgling stage and still needed a lot of input for developing proper infrastructure and promoting it in the right way. She immediately set about trying to improve the staid and synthetic look of the tourist bungalows that came under her consideration. She had seen and lived in the best palaces in the country and although she was not expecting these bungalows to measure up to those standards, when she saw the rooms she was quite shocked by their tasteless décor. Given her innate sense of style, the interiors of these tourist bungalows seemed very tacky to her. She knew very well that she was dealing with people who hadn't a clue about interior decoration or proper use of space. "I wasn't trying to turn these bungalows into palaces but sometimes there were little things that only needed a bit of common sense. Simple things like placing doormats and side tables, getting the right curtains and a proper whitewash also became an uphill task." She remembers, "You know I wasn't being too critical but sometimes it did seem quite frustrating trying to get these basic jobs understood."

She continued to take great interest in her job, attending office and dealing with bemused officers who didn't really know how to interact with the Rajmata, used as they were to dealing with the usual bureaucrat. Despite her short tenure she gave it her undivided attention and hoped she had made a difference in their approach. "Do you know I was the cheapest Chairperson that RTDC has ever had," she smiles. "I just cost them a *lakh* of rupees in the entire year that I held that post. Now people are spending more than that every month!"

Another area where she continued to make a huge difference was as a patron of arts and crafts. She had always promoted craftsmen of the state and had single-handedly revived the dying craft of blue pottery and given a new life to the famed block printing industry of Sanganer. She sent craftsmen for training and gave them a much-needed platform through her Shri Chand Shilp Shala, a craft school that encouraged underprivileged women to learn some skills that they could use to earn an extra income.

In May 1978, her son Jagat married Priyanandana Rangsit, a Thai princess, which kept her occupied for a while. She had also shifted her residence from Rajmahal to Moti Doongri and now to the smaller Lily Pool, located close to Rambagh Palace, her first home in Jaipur.

She still had much to keep her busy. There was the City Palace Museum that needed to be managed, MGD Girls School had an excellent Principal but it was her personal interest that made all the difference. She visited it often, talking to teachers, inviting well-known people from varied fields to interact with the students, and encouraging them to perform better in every sphere of life.

Much had changed over the years and for the younger generation royalty and their stories were things of the past; merely something that their mothers and grandmothers talked about when they discussed the 'good old days'. But not so with the dynamic Rajmata Gayatri Devi; in her case it was almost as if time had stood still for her. Her charm, her dignity, her grace and her understated yet forceful personality made her the most sought after and admired person in Jaipur. Every single day there are requests from newspapers and magazines for interviews, requests to inaugurate exhibitions, to be chief guest at some institute or to bless a newly married couple. Her office in Lily Pool is always open to people, anybody can walk in and meet her and discuss his or her problems with her. She continues to be the *annadata*, or provider, that she has always been and it wasn't a new role that she had taken on herself. She was born and brought up that way and it did not matter that the Government had taken away their titles, she was above all that. She was still the Rajmata for everyone.

Your Royal Highness,

We have so many things to say thank you for that it is virtually impossible to express them in a few chosen words.

Since the inception of this school we have been looking upon you for guidance, for inspiration, for support.

Each time, each day, every little nuance of M.G.D. is a reflection of your dream. And every passing year — the achievement of that dream.

So, Thank you your highness, for everything.

The M.G.D family..

261 Maharani Gayatri Devi Girls Public School, the school that she started in August 1943, was always very close to her heart and she took a keen interest in all their activities. Picture on the left shows a letter written by the students and staff of the school and on the right Rajmata being received at a school function.

262 and 263 In the late 1980s Rajmata Gayatri Devi turned her attention towards updating a cookbook that she had compiled in 1969. Picture shows a page from her notebook where she had jotted down her foreword for the new edition of her book. Picture on the right shows Rajmata Gayatri Devi holding a copy of her bestselling autobiography *A Princess Remembers*.

In the years that followed she felt the need to start another school. There had been a demand from the citizens of Jaipur that they needed a co-educational school, and given the excellent reputation of her previous school, everybody thought that she was the best person to start it. Also, there were no good English medium schools in Jaipur. She started not one but two more schools: the Maharaja Sawai Maharaja Man Singh Vidyalaya as the much needed co-educational school, and another one just outside Jaipur called the Lalitya Bal Niketan, named after her granddaughter, Jagat's daughter. This was located in a small village because her driver said there was no school in his village and children had to go to another village for basic education.

Jagat, her only son, died in 1997 at the age of 48, and the months that followed found her in a rather depressed state of mind. She talked of death and of having lived too long. "It was a terrible loss when my beloved, darling son Jagat passed away. It is something that I cannot get over. And I often wonder had I taken more care of him he might still have been with us today. He was such a good-looking, charming, intelligent person and very popular with everybody, he was generous to a fault. I shall never forget seeing him lying on his bed in the hospital, not breathing and I knew Jagat was no more. I cannot describe the pain of this moment and every now and then it comes back and I blame myself and I wonder about life and death." It was sad to see her like that but one could only watch from the sidelines and do little to ease the sorrow and pain that she was obviously going through.

A year later I edited and published the *Gourmet's Gateway*. It surprised all of us by doing well. It also amused people that two non-cooks had put this book together! While working on the book she discussed the possibilities of doing other books as well. Why not a book on Jaipur? Or better still, why not another biography? A book with Rajmata Gayatri Devi of Jaipur? It gave me an opportunity to meet her on a more regular basis and also all the people who had been in close contact with her. Little known gems about the pranks that she played on unsuspecting guests, her consideration for people and her efforts to put people at ease came out very clearly in the interviews.

Her sense of humor and her love for gossip make her seem more humane. She can pull one's leg so subtly that it takes most people a while to realize that they've been had! One has to know her well enough to see through her jokes. Once she was invited for dinner. Among the guests were some non-Jaipur people who did not know who she was. The lady asked for an introduction. Without batting an eyelid Rajmata Sahiba said, "Oh, I'm a doctor from a nearby hospital and this gentleman here is my assistant. Now, if you'll excuse us we have to go for an operation." The 'assistant' nearly choked on his drink but quickly regained his composure and accompanied the 'lady doctor' to assist in the operation!

She can say the most unexpected thing with such a straight face that one doesn't know whether to laugh or be shocked. I remember sitting in her office and one of her secretaries was absent. She asked the office assistant, in a very serious tone, *"Kya wo mar gaye hain?"* (Is he dead?)! The poor man just shook his head and looked down. She loves to put people in embarrassing situations. Rajmata has put me in a tight spot several times. Once she introduced me to somebody with, "Oh, this is Dharmendar and she doesn't like you. She thinks you're not an honest person!" The man, whom I was meeting for the first time, looked quite confused and suitably hurt. The next few minutes were embarrassing for me as I tried to extract myself from the awkward situation while Rajmata Sahiba looked on, very pleased with herself, enjoying every minute of my discomfiture.

For a woman of the world she is very trusting and quite gullible. She has lost several rare photographs because some smooth talking businessperson has talked her into parting with pictures from her private collection. She often introduces people as "my very good (sometimes 'old') friend" but doesn't have a clue as to who they are. Ask her their name and she'll give a name even the 'old friend' has never heard of!

264–265 and 265 Mrs. Jacqueline Kennedy Onassis was a personal friend of Rajmata Gayatri Devi and visited Jaipur again as editor with Doubleday and Company. She edited books for several exhibitions at the Costume Institute that included *Costumes of Royal India* (1985). She is seen here with Rajmata Gayatri Devi at Rambagh.

266, 266–267 and 267 The Jaipur royal family's links with the British Royals continued unbroken and they remained in regular touch. Rajmata's interest in the game of polo continued and she always attended the polo season in England when she was there. Pictures show her with Prince Charles (in England and in India) and the Duke of Edinburgh (bottom, second from left). Prince Charles visited Jaipur and is given a traditional welcome in Lilypool, the Rajmata's last residence.

While working on this book I came to expect her calls each day at around 11.30am and I made sure that my mornings were always free for her. The phone would ring and the unmistakable voice on the other end would ask "Dharmendar, what are you doing? Are you very busy? Can you come over?" Sometimes I wasn't just recording her reminiscences, it would be either a letter that had to be written to the Government, or else some information that she wanted. Of course, the session often ended in catching up on the gossip. She loves to gossip and I learnt after several months that one had to be very careful when giving her any information because it would often come back with a "Rajmata Sahib said that you'd told her that M was interested in P…" or some such shocker.

While working on the book it was necessary to pull out all the old photographs and very soon the huge dining table was full of old albums that had been displayed there for selection. She asked me, tongue in cheek, "Dharmendar, when will I have my table back?! I think it will be nice to eat on the dining table!" I assured her that it would only take me a few days to go through the albums and then I'd have all the albums moved out of the way. She said, "No don't worry. We can manage quite well on the small table."

But she is like that, one of the most considerate and caring people I have known. I have also watched her in the middle of a hot summer day patiently posing for pictures in the garden, even putting the nervous photographer at ease by following his instructions without a word of complaint and without asking him to hurry up with the shooting. I have watched the concern she has shown for her ADC who had accompanied her to a new city. She herself was unwell but ensured that he was taken sightseeing and to the right shops to pick up gifts for his family.

You feel her charisma from a distance even through photographs, but when she turns her compassion and caring towards one personally then you sense the depth of her character. During the course of our various meetings I told Rajmata Sahiba that I was having some problems with my job and that I would have to leave if things did not work out satisfactorily. She wanted to know all the details about the how and why and I told her in as few words as possible. She wasn't really surprised when I said that I needed to go away somewhere. I like to think that I saw a little sympathy in her eyes. She did not say it in so many words but I could see that she wanted to reassure me. I must have looked quite stricken. All I said was that I needed some excuse to go away for a few days because it was becoming quite awkward for me to be in town and she immediately said, "All right, we'll go away to Sawai Madhopur. You can come with me."

Those were the days when I was feeling very low and depressed, and her words touched me so much that I couldn't stop the tears in my eyes. Here was this great lady, brought up in a way that she had very little time for other people and their little day-to-day problems, who was quite used to having people run around after her, and she had been sensitive enough to understand that I was feeling quite low. She did not have to say anything about the problems that I was facing, she did not discuss the right and wrong of the situation but she knew instinctively that it was upsetting for me. And she cared enough to say those kind words to make me feel better.

269 The Rajmata has always been in great demand for interviews and photo shoots. This is a formal portrait of Rajmata Gayatri Devi, taken by a Japanese photographer for use in a magazine interview.

270 Rajmata Gayatri Devi has a special fondness for Sawai Madhopur and often provides finances for various relevant community activities. Here she inaugurates one such structure while the villagers look on.

I have traveled with her several times, to Calcutta, Cooch Behar, Sawai Madhopur, Mumbai, Hampi, Amritsar, Delhi and Lahore (Pakistan), and have always been amazed by the response she elicits; the look of awe in people's eyes is difficult to describe. Rajmata looks so serene and graceful that it is easy to understand the great admiration in those surrounding her.

People who've had the honor and privilege of knowing her realize that she is not only sensitive but cares for people and their feelings. She would call me to Lily Pool after that almost every day to discuss some aspect of the book, and it helped settle my mind to a great extent. The fact that she also called me to escort her to various functions also helped divert my mind from my problems. This was a period in my life that would have been a little more difficult to live through without her kindness.

Her concern about the state of affairs in the city also extends to her hometown Cooch Behar which she visits regularly and takes great interest in welfare activities there for which she arranges funds. For the people of Cooch Behar she is *Amader Rajkumari*, our princess, and whenever she

visits her home town she is surrounded by hundreds of people wanting to see her and talk to her and share their problems with her. No matter how tired she is – nothing can keep her from meeting these people who come from miles away to see her. On her last trip she happily visited her brother's old ADC and joined his family for a meal in their one-room house. There was no discomfiture and she thoroughly enjoyed the simple meal that the family had put together.

In Jaipur she never refuses an invitation, especially if it comes from some poor villager. I remember accompanying her on one such occasion. The first thing she said when she saw me was, "We're going for a grand engagement ceremony." I wasn't dressed appropriately so I said I'm sorry I didn't know. She said it didn't really matter. On the way she asked her ADC if they'd serve champagne. The ADC just looked on politely and refused to comment. All I said was I didn't know it was that kind of an event. She just smiled mysteriously. Along the way she said, "I hope your stomach is okay?" I assured her that it was. She said, "Good. Because they're going to

271 Rajmata Gayatri Devi as the chief guest at an army function.

give us something to eat, I'm not going to eat so you'll have to eat otherwise it will not look nice…!" I just laughed and thanked her.

We reached the farm of the villager whose grandson was getting engaged. There were people waiting on the road to receive her and there was excitement in the air as the car drove in. People surged towards the car to get a glimpse of her and there was a line of people who came to touch her feet and seek her blessings. She slowly made her way through the crowd and sat on the cane chair that had been put for her. The sweets arrived and I of course ended up eating them! She called an old *tonga wala* and chatted with him about the old times. He complained about the rising prices and the fact that things were so much better during the days of the maharajas and that the politicians were all out to make money and only showed their faces during elections. She enjoyed chatting with them and when it was time to leave she went over to the women's section and chatted with a few more of them.

When it was time to leave we were all given 50 rupees as a token. On the drive back she said, "Why have they given us money?" When the ADC explained that it was a custom to give this to the boy's side of the family, she counted the money and said, with almost child-like glee, "Then I'm going again!" The way she said it was so funny that we all burst out laughing.

Rajmata Gayatri Devi has led a full life with few regrets. If she had to live again she would like to be reborn as Maharani Gayatri Devi of Jaipur. She had all the luxuries that are part and parcel of a royal background; an acknowledged beauty who could very well have settled to a life of parties and politics. She is a much interviewed, photographed and written-about lady even today and could have spent the rest of her life basking in past glory. But she chose to blaze a path where none existed. She made it her mission in life to liberate women from *purdah* and she gave countless women a chance to take their own place in the sun. Whenever historians talk about the emancipation of women, Rajmata's name will have to be written in golden letters.

272 and 273 A fond grandmother – Rajmata Gayatri Devi's only son Maharaj Jagat Singh had two children Lalitya Kumari and Devraj Singh. She is seen here celebrating the birthdays of her grandchildren.

274 and 275 The colorful Indian festival of Holi was a time of great fun and revelry. Family members and close friends were invited to Lilypool to participate in the festivities; there was music, color and food as participants tried to apply color on each other.

Another cause very dear to her is the preservation of her beloved pink city. The destruction of the city causes her immense pain and she tries to bring this to the notice of the authorities regularly. "But who are the people today that you can go to? Nobody. The city is being destroyed by haphazard, unplanned growth. I wish the Government would do something to rectify some of the mistakes that have been made over the years. It makes me sad to see the ruination of such a beautiful city." There is a lot of heartfelt pain in her voice when she says, "The city was such a joy to behold. Its architecture was unique. His Highness once told me that whatever we are, we are because of Jaipur and whatever we have we must give back to Jaipur. Times have changed, he has gone, Jagat has gone too, but I am still here and I try my best to do whatever I can for Jaipur. It is very heartbreaking for me to see this once beautiful place deteriorating so rapidly in front of my eyes."

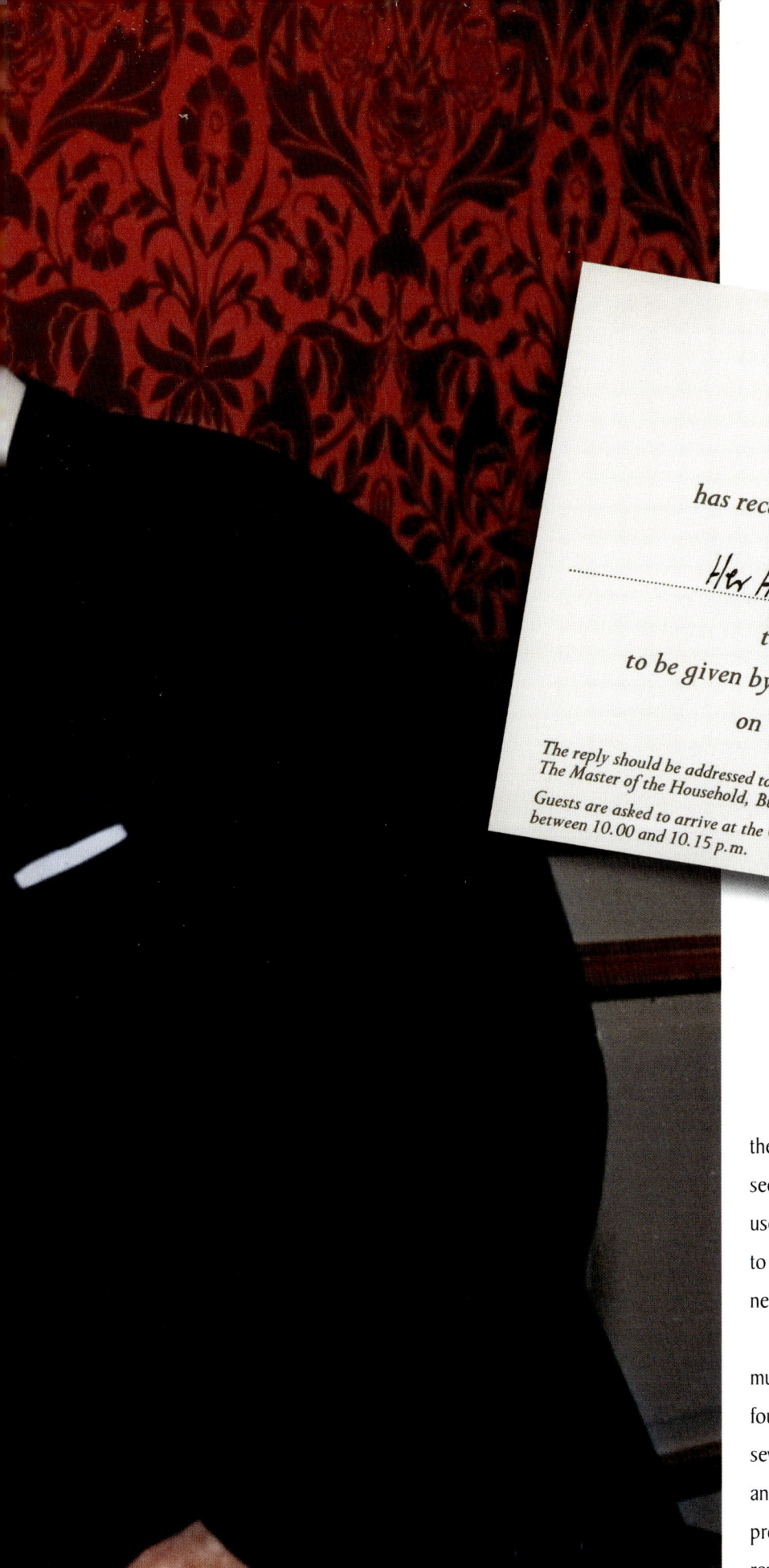

278–279 and 279 The graceful Rajamata Gayatri Devi of Jaipur being welcomed by the Duke of Edinburgh at a formal function at Windsor Castle. Right is an invitation card from Her Majesty the Queen.

EⁱⁱR

The Master of the Household
has received Her Majesty's command to invite

Her Highness the Rajmata of Jaipur

to a Dance at Windsor Castle
to be given by The Queen and The Duke of Edinburgh
on Wednesday, 18th June, 1986

The reply should be addressed to:
The Master of the Household, Buckingham Palace

Guests are asked to arrive at the Castle
between 10.00 and 10.15 p.m.

Dress:
Black Tie

She is a patron of the World Wildlife Fund and takes keen interest in their activities. Her long-standing interest in the preservation of wildlife sees her visiting her once favorite hunting ground – Ranthambhore. She uses her rich and influential friends overseas to raise funds for causes dear to her heart. Several schools for the handicapped and institutions for the needy have benefited from her philanthropic activities.

Rani Vidya Devi, her daughter-in-law says, "I have often felt that too much emphasis on her beauty has tended to overshadow her more profound side. Her significant contributions to society include the funding of several leading educational institutions, charitable trusts, her patronage and active encouragement to animal welfare organizations, her efforts to preserve heritage are just a few of the lasting facets of her life which will remain forever in the minds of people."

280 top Rajmata Gayatri Devi is known for her interest in the preservation of the heritage of her beloved city and is always available to lend her support where needed. Picture shows her joining protestors who were demonstrating against the felling of trees. (Author Dharmendar Kanwar is on her left).

280 bottom Rajmata Gayatri Devi is a patron of an institute for the physically challenged and is always there to encourage and support the students in all their activities. Picture shows her during a function of that institute.

280-281 It has been a custom in Jaipur that all functions related to birthdays and religious ceremonies always started from the *zenana*, or the ladies' section of the palace. Picture shows Rajmata Gayatri Devi in her section of *Zenani Deori* on her 80th birthday.

282 and 283 Photograph from the Arisia Diamond Collection advertising campaign (left). Even today Rajmata Gayatri Devi is in great demand to promote jewellery and saris. She is a much-loved and respected Rajmata and there is always a great deal of interest in her well-being. Letters, cards, flowers pour in when people hear of her illness. When the Jaipur heat becomes unbearable, she moves to her home in London and spends the summer months there. She is seen here relaxing in her London home.

Life goes on and in the last few years she has had a few minor (and major) operations and faced them with her usual fortitude. She still sits in her office every single day answering letters, meeting people, attending functions. Nothing has changed except that her mobility is not what it used to be, but the spirit remains unbroken. She is a real princess who still does things properly with all her inborn style and grace. Today, the years have created delicate lines of age across her face. She still retains her old charm and

grace and is a much sought after celebrity across the country – and abroad.

She is relieved that the tension she had with her eldest stepson Maharaja Brig. Bhawani Singh is now a thing of the past. "I am happy that we did not have any tension between us now because we were always a very close family."

She says, "I have no regrets. I've done whatever I wanted to do but I want to tidy everything before I leave."

284 top left Rajmata visited the Golden Temple in Amritsar when she was on her way to Lahore, Pakistan for a polo match. Picture shows her coming out of the temple.

284 top right Rajmata had a deep attachment and love for the people of Cooch Behar and tried to visit her hometown at least once a year. Picture shows her at a religious function in Cooch Behar.

284 bottom Celebrating her 89th birthday in Lilypool, her residence in Jaipur. Helping her is her daughter-in-law Maharani Vidya Devi, wife of Maharaj Jai Singh.

285 The Rajmata in her office in Jaipur, with pictures of family members in the background.

286 The DeBeers "Arisia" Diamond range was launched in Mumbai in a well-attended function. Rajmata Gayatri Devi was the brand ambassador and unveiled a special collection of jewelry. These stamps were produced on that occasion.

This book would not have possible without the help and support of late Her Highness Rajmata Gayatri Devi of Jaipur. She was very generous with her time and patiently went through the photographs and identified them for this book. Her childlike enthusiasm made the, sometimes tedious, job rather pleasant. I would like to dedicate this book to this wonderful lady, a legend in her lifetime and an incredible role model for countless people.

I would also like to thank other members of the Jaipur royal family - Maharaj Jai Singh and Rani Vidya Devi, Maharaj Prithviraj Singh and the late Rani Devika Devi for their help when I needed to cross check something or identify someone. They made my job so much easier.

A big "Thank You" to my two in-house sub editors — my husband Kr. N.P. Singh and my son Abhijit Singh who read and re-read the ms and made several valid suggestions. I would like to thank Sudhir Kasliwal and the wonderful White Star team for their assistance and support.

Dharmendar Kanwar

WHITE STAR PUBLISHERS

WS White Star Publishers® is a registered trademark
property of Edizioni White Star s.r.l.

© 2009 Edizioni White Star s.r.l.
Via Candido Sassone, 24
13100 Vercelli, Italy
www.whitestar.it

Editing: Jane Pamenter

ISBN 978-88-544-0494-6

1 2 3 4 5 6   13 12 11 10 09

Printed in Italy